As For Me and My *Spouse* We Will Praise The Lord

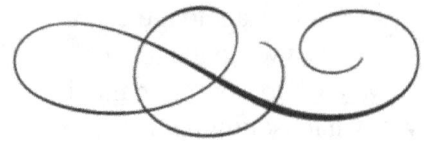

Harrison S. Mungal

Foreword by Jachin Mullen

As For Me And My Spouse We Will Praise The Lord

Copyright © 2025 Harrison S. Mungal
All rights reserved. Neither this publication nor any part of this publication may be reproduced or transmitted in any form or by any means, electronic or mechanical, including photocopying, recording or any information storage and retrieval system, without permission in writing from the author.

Unless otherwise identified, Scripture quotations are from New King James Version of the Bible.

Contact author via email:
hsmungal@hotmail.com
info@agetoage.ca
www.agetoage.ca
www.harrisonmungal.com
www.harrisonmungalbooks.com
Facebook: Harrison Mungal
Twitter: AgeToAgeInc1
LinkedIn: Harrison Mungal, Ph.D., PsyD
YouTube: Harrison Mungal
Phone: 905-533-1334

ABOUT the AUTHOR

Harrison Sharma Mungal, *BTh, MCC, MSW, PhD, PsyD*

Dr. Mungal is a devoted therapist with a background in mental health and clinical psychology, driven by a genuine passion for life and the well-being of those under his care. With an impressive literary portfolio comprising over 50 books and a seasoned public speaking career that has reached audiences in over 53 nations, he brings a wealth of knowledge and skills to his practice.

Alongside his professional accomplishments, Dr. Mungal places a high value on family, with a successful marriage of over 35 years, seven children, and multiple grandchildren. In addition to his clinical practice, Dr. Mungal and his wife have played pivotal roles in church planting, pastoral ministry, and missionary work, even during the challenging times of the Cold War in Croatia from 1994-1997. They have nurtured congregations, established churches, and served as missionaries, demonstrating a deep commitment to spreading the gospel. Their dedication extended to running a Bible college, Metro Bible College, for over a decade before transitioning into mental health and addictions counselling.

Dr. Mungal is widely respected for his unique ability to blend biblical principles with scientific insights, adding a distinctive "psychology twist" to his therapeutic approach. He explained God made us Body, Soul (mind, will and emotions) and Spirit. As much as people need support physically and spiritually, "the soul is where people are wounded and is in need of healing." His expertise has been sought after by various media outlets, including appearances on television programs including 700 Clubs Canada and 100 Huntly St. He has also been invited to speak at prestigious institutions such as the Attorney General of Canada, police departments, hospitals, community agencies, and churches. His contributions have earned him accolades and recognition from local authorities, police departments, mayors, community leaders, and countless families.

With over 21 years of experience in mental health, psychiatry, and psychology, coupled with over four decades dedicated to teaching and preaching the gospel, Dr. Mungal possesses a wealth of expertise in both fields. His educational background is equally impressive, with a Christian Leadership Certificate, a Ministerial Diploma from two years of Bible College, a bachelor's degree in Theology, two master's degrees (in Counselling and Social Work), and two doctorate degrees (in Social Work and Clinical Psychology).

In summary, Dr. Mungal's journey is a testament to his unwavering commitment to serving others, integrating his faith with his professional expertise to make a positive impact in the lives of countless individuals, couples, and families. His multifaceted career reflects a deep sense of purpose and a profound dedication to promoting holistic healing and spiritual growth.

ABOUT
HARRISON *and* KATHLEEN

Harrison and Kathleen Mungal have built their lives on a foundation of faith, love, and a deep commitment to family. With over 35 years of a strong and successful marriage, they have nurtured a beautiful family that includes seven children, in-laws, and multiple grandchildren. Their devotion to the Lord is at the heart of their journey, and they actively serve in their local churches, carrying forward their passion for ministry.

Together, Harrison and Kathleen have played pivotal roles in church planting, pastoral leadership, and missionary work. As missionaries during the War in Croatia from 1994 to 1997, they ministered in challenging circumstances, spreading the gospel with unwavering faith. Over the years, they pastored in four churches, planted two congregations, and established a Bible college, which they led for over a decade. Their transition into mental health and addictions counseling was a natural extension of their heart for healing, combining their pastoral experience with practical tools to support individuals and families.

Their ministry spans the globe, speaking in churches worldwide on topics related to relationships, marriage, parenting, mental health, addictions, and the intersection of spirituality and psychology. Harrison is widely respected for his ability to blend biblical truths with scientific insights, bringing a unique "psychology twist" to his therapeutic approach. He explains that God created us as Body, Soul (mind, will, and emotions), and Spirit, and while physical and spiritual support are crucial, "the soul is where people are wounded and is in need of healing."

Harrison's expertise has been sought after by numerous media outlets, including appearances on *700 Club Canada* and *100 Huntley Street*. His wisdom has been shared in prestigious institutions, such as the Attorney General of Canada, police departments, hospitals, community agencies, and churches. His contributions have earned him widespread recognition from local authorities, police departments, mayors, community leaders, and countless families.

Through their life's work, Harrison and Kathleen have demonstrated an unwavering commitment to service—integrating faith, wisdom, and compassion to positively impact individuals, couples, and families. Their journey stands as a testament to the power of love, faith, and the pursuit of healing for those in need.

FOREWORD by
JACHIN MULLEN

As you read this book, you'll quickly discover that Harrison Mungal is a unique gift to you, a friend to your marriage, family life and spiritual walk with God. Harrison brings together a blend of brilliance, psychology, spirituality and practical wisdom. What makes this even more powerful is that his insights are not just theoretical—they are lived. He embodies the very principles he teaches, offering a life that serves as a model worth following. That kind of integrity is rare, and it makes this book not only worth reading but worth treasuring.

The principles of praise that Harrison shares will serve as a guide through both the great times and difficult times in your journey. Praise becomes a breakthrough when you choose to trust God in every season.

You might look at Harrison's photo and think he's in his early thirties, but he and his wonderful wife, Kathleen, have been married for 35 years. Together, they've raised seven children and now enjoy the blessing of two grandchildren. Out of that experience he will share with you some secrets of how to keep your marriage moving forward through the mountain seasons but also the dark valley seasons as you keep praise your priority. You will find that this will be of great benefit to you and your spouse but will also effect your whole family.

There are books that inform, books that inspire, and then there are books that awaken something deep within the soul. *As for Me and My Spouse, We Will Praise the Lord* is one such book. It is not merely a collection of stories or reflections—it is a living testimony, a sacred offering of praise forged in the fires of real life.

As a pastor, I have walked with many through seasons of joy and sorrow, faith and doubt. I have seen how praise can be both a celebration and a sacrifice. What you hold in your hands is a powerful reminder that worship is not confined to the walls of a sanctuary—it is a way of life, a declaration of trust in the goodness of God even when the path is steep and the answers are few.

The authors of this book have lived what they write. Their journey is marked not by ease, but by endurance; not by perfection, but by perseverance. Through grief, sickness, loss, and uncertainty, they have chosen to lift their voices in praise. And in doing so, they have discovered a truth that resonates far beyond their own story: that worship is a weapon, a refuge, and a lifeline. As Harrison says, "Kathleen and I built our marriage on praise and worship, it was not a ritual or obligation, but a lifeline."

This book is a call to courage. It invites every reader to step into a deeper kind of faith—a faith that praises not because of what is seen, but because of who God is. It challenges us to worship not only in the light, but in the shadows; not only in victory, but in the valley.

Whether you are in a season of celebration or struggle, these pages will meet you where you are. They will remind you that God is near, that His presence is real, and that praise is always possible. May this book stir your spirit, strengthen your faith, and lead you into a deeper encounter with the One who is always worthy.

Jachin Mullen
Lead Pastor, Home Church

ABOUT JACHIN MULLEN

Jachin Mullen is the kind of person who makes you feel like you've known him forever, even if you've just met. As the lead pastor of Home Church, a thriving multi-site family with over 120 locations worldwide, he pours his heart into preaching the gospel and leading people into a deeper, life-changing relationship with Jesus. His passion isn't just in words—it's in the way he connects, the way he welcomes, the way he loves.

A gifted musician, Jachin has written and recorded songs with Integrity Music, Maranatha Music, and even produced several of his own projects. His love for worship is woven into every part of his life, bringing joy and inspiration to those around him.

But beyond his ministry and music, his greatest joy is found in his family. Alongside his wife, Becca, he is raising their four amazing children in Red Deer, Alberta, where serving God together is not just a calling—it's a way of life. Their home is filled with laughter, love, and a shared enthusiasm for sports. Whether cheering on the Edmonton Oilers, Los Angeles Chargers, or Los Angeles Clippers, Jachin brings the same fiery passion to the game that he brings to his faith.

If you step into Home Church on a Sunday morning, you won't have to look far to find him. He'll be at the front door, greeting everyone with a warm handshake, a heartfelt smile, and a genuine love for every person who walks through those doors. Whether it's in the church or out in the community, his heart is always to encourage, uplift, and share God's unfailing love.

Jachin lives with joy, excitement, and a true appreciation for the beauty of life. He celebrates big moments and small victories alike, making every day an opportunity to glorify God. When you hear him speak, you'll not only be inspired—you'll feel empowered to step boldly into what God has called you to do. His enthusiasm is contagious, his faith unshakable, and his love for people undeniable.

Jachin is more than a pastor, more than a leader—he is a living example of what it means to walk humbly with God, to love unconditionally, and to inspire faith in every heart he touches. From the moment you meet him, you sense something different, something profound. It's not just his passion for people or his unwavering dedication to sharing Jesus—it's the undeniable presence of God that radiates through his life.

Our friendship began through his father, pastor Mel Mullen who was instrumental in sending Kathleen and I and our 3 three children to Croatian in 1994. Our friendship quickly became something deeper—a bond built on trust, faith, and an unshakable commitment to God's calling. From the very first encounter of meeting Jachin, it was evident that he doesn't just talk about the love of Jesus; he lives it. His heart is open, his humility is genuine, and his kindness is unwavering.

As a mentor, a role model, and a confidant, Jachin carries the nature of God in every word, every action, every moment. He walks alongside others not as someone who seeks recognition, but as a servant-leader who lifts others up, who sees their potential, and who encourages them to step fully into the purpose God has set before them. Whether through a heartfelt conversation or a powerful sermon, he imparts wisdom, strength, and an unrelenting hope that transforms lives.

I count it as an incredible blessing to be a part of his life, to witness firsthand the miracles, the movements, the transformative work God is accomplishing through him. His faithfulness to God's call is inspiring, his heart is steadfast, and his love for people is boundless. To know Jachin is to know what it means to lead with love, to serve with joy, and to walk in the fullness of what God has in store. And through it all, he remains exactly as he has always been—a friend, a mentor, and a reflection of God's grace.

Table of Contents

INTRODUCTION 13
GRIEF'S SILENT CRY 17
IN THE FACE OF FEAR 33
THE PRELUDE TO PASSION 43
SPARKS BEFORE THE FLAME 53
WHEN TWO HEARTS SING 61
PRAISE UNVEILED 77
THE HEARTBEAT OF HEAVEN 89
PRAISING HIM IN THE STORM 107
SILENT HEARTS 115
UNLEASHING HEAVEN'S POWER 121
LAYING THE GROUNDWORK 133
AS FOR ME AND MY SPOUSE WE WILL PRAISE THE LORD! .. 141
A MARRIAGE ROOTED IN PRAISE 149
CONCLUSION 153

INTRODUCTION

There are moments in life when praise feels effortless, when the joy of the Lord overflows, filling every breath, every heartbeat, every step. And then there are moments when praise requires every ounce of strength, when faith is tested in the fires of grief, loss, and uncertainty. This book is not just a reflection of our journey but an offering of testimony—an unwavering declaration that through every trial and triumph, as for me and my spouse, we will praise the Lord.

Our story is not one of perfection. It is not one of a smooth path laid out before us without obstacles. No, it is a story of deep valleys and breathtaking peaks, of moments when the light of God felt distant and others when His presence was undeniable. It is the story of love, faith, and a commitment to worship—not only in the comfort of sanctuary walls but in the rawness of life's hardships.

I remember the day I met Kathleen, the way our journey began not in romance but in shared faith. It was a simple encounter, yet it carried the weight of divine purpose. The Holy Spirit spoke, whispering a truth that would shape my life forever: *She is your wife.* At the time, I laughed—not out of disbelief, but out of sheer wonder. How easily God can take the ordinary—two strangers meeting in church—and transform

INTRODUCTION

it into something extraordinary. That was the beginning of our journey, a foundation laid in praise, built upon trust in His guidance.

But there would come times when praise would not come as easily. When grief knocked at my door, stealing the presence of a dear friend, I wrestled with God in silent sorrow. The pain felt unbearable, and for a moment, my worship wavered. How do you praise when your heart is aching? How do you lift your hands when they tremble under the weight of loss? And yet, it was in those moments that I learned the deepest truth about praise—it is not dependent on circumstance, but on the unwavering goodness of God.

Faith was tested in other ways, too. Living as Protestants in Croatia brought challenges that threatened our peace. There were days of unease, moments where fear knocked at the edges of our hearts. But even then, praise remained our refuge, a shield against the voices that sought to intimidate us. Worship was not just an act; it was a weapon, an anchor in a storm that tried to shake us.

I think back to the day we returned from India, weary but hopeful, only to find our van stolen—along with boxes of carved elephants we had brought back as gifts. The frustration, the loss, the questions—all of it threatened to steal my gratitude. Why would God allow this? Wasn't our mission good, our hearts surrendered? But through the haze of disappointment, praise still broke through. Worship is never about what we have or what we lose, but about the One who remains constant through it all.

There were seasons of sickness when my body was weak and my heart questioned. I watched Kathleen stand strong, her faith unwavering, her prayers calling down heaven to rescue us. It was in those moments that I saw the power of praise—not only in lifting our spirits but in shifting the very atmosphere of our lives. When we worship, we invite heaven to move, to intervene, to pour out the presence of God in ways beyond our comprehension.

AS FOR ME AND MY SPOUSE WE WILL PRAISE THE LORD

Through every trial, every moment of doubt, praise has remained our testimony. It has been our choice, our commitment, our declaration of trust in the One who holds our every breath. And as we stand today, reflecting on the years of love, loss, victory, and surrender, our anthem remains the same: as for me and my spouse, we will praise the Lord.

This book is an invitation. It is a call to every heart that has wrestled with faith, that has questioned in seasons of pain, that has rejoiced in moments of breakthrough. May these pages be a reminder that no matter the storm, no matter the valley, no matter the darkness that threatens to overwhelm—praise is always the answer. Worship is the sound of heaven, the language of faith, the declaration of hope. And in every season, through every moment, may we all find the courage to lift our voices and declare His goodness.

There have been days where praise came as a sacrifice, where lifting our voices required fighting through fear, doubt, and exhaustion. There were moments in sickness, uncertainty, financial struggles, and disappointments when everything in us wanted to withdraw. But God is never absent. His faithfulness is unchanging, His love unwavering. And when we make the choice to worship Him even through our weakness, we experience the miracle of His presence.

I have learned that praise is not only a response to blessing but also an act of defiance against despair. It is an offering that declares: *God is still good, even when life feels unfair.* Kathleen and I have faced valleys, times of great loss, and seasons of uncertainty, but through every one of them, praise has been our lifeline. It has carried us through the deepest waters, held us steady in the fiercest winds, and reminded us that we are never alone.

As I reflect on our journey, I see the fingerprints of God in every chapter. I see His grace woven into our marriage, His mercy carrying us through trials, His promises sustaining us even when we doubted. This book is not just a retelling of our story—it is a testimony of what

INTRODUCTION

happens when two hearts commit to praising God no matter what. It is a witness to the power of worship, the strength it brings, and the breakthrough it unlocks.

There will be seasons when praise requires effort, when faith is tested, when answers seem distant. But there is one truth that remains: *God is always worthy of our praise.* And so, with every breath, with every moment we are given, we will lift His name high. We will declare His goodness, trust in His promises, and celebrate His faithfulness.

Our marriage was built on praise, and it will endure through worship. It is our greatest joy, our deepest conviction, and the foundation on which we stand. And so, as for me and my spouse, we will praise the Lord.

GRIEF'S SILENT CRY

People often ask, "Would you do it again?" They wonder if, knowing what I know now—the struggles, the pain, the losses—I would still make the choice to take my family, three young children, into a war-torn country. Would I still go to serve people who were not my own, knowing full well that I could have lost everything? My answer has never changed. Yes, I would do it again.

There is nothing I would alter when it comes to the call God placed on my heart. Though there are regrets, moments I wish had unfolded differently, and pains that will never fully leave me, I would still choose to go. Even knowing the obstacles that met us at every turn, the heartache that weighed us down, and even the loss of my best friend, Tihomir, I would still go back. Because serving God, loving His people, and walking in obedience have never been about comfort or ease—they have been about faith. And faith has always sustained us.

Tihomir was, and always will be, one of the most incredible souls I have ever known. Meeting him felt like encountering a piece of heaven itself. He wasn't just a friend; he was like an angel placed in our path, meant to walk alongside Kathleen and me during one of the most uncertain seasons of our lives.

I met Tihomir on my first trip to Croatia in October of 1994. His life was at a crossroads—a moment of searching, of longing, of deciding which path to take. His friends had pushed him toward the world, taking him to sleep with a prostitute. But even as he stood there, faced with temptation, something deep inside him rebelled. He couldn't do it. He walked away, uncertain of where to go, lost in thought, seeking something more.

And then, he stumbled upon a bookstore. His eyes landed on a Bible, and something stirred within him. He bought it, though he barely knew why. He began reading it, even as he studied law, preparing to become a lawyer. And in this season of transition, someone introduced him to me.

From the moment we met, I could sense his hunger, his yearning for something greater than the life he had known. I told him about the Holy Spirit, about how He had been my closest companion—my ever-present guide and comfort. I shared with him how Jesus had changed everything for me, how the love of God had transformed my very being.

That night, we walked for hours, discussing God, salvation, purpose and my relationship with the Holy Spirit. It was one of the most powerful nights of my life. I watched as the love of Jesus consumed him—watched as his heart softened, as understanding took root.

He dropped me off at my apartment, but I knew something had changed in him. And the next day, when he met me again, he confirmed it. He hadn't been able to sleep. Our conversation had taken hold of his heart, refusing to let go. And there, in the quiet of his room, he had knelt and surrendered himself fully to Jesus.

Joy flooded me, an overwhelming gratitude for the way God moves, for the way He reaches into even the most unexpected places to pull people toward His love.

From that moment on, Tihomir was insatiable in his pursuit of Jesus. He couldn't learn enough, couldn't ask enough questions, couldn't satisfy the hunger in his soul to understand the depth of what Christ had done.

When I returned to Canada that year, on my way home, Tihomir reached out, asking if I could buy him a Bible. His English was minimal at the time, yet through the help of translations and the shared language of faith, we understood each other. There was something profound about his request—it wasn't merely about owning a book, but about seeking truth, about filling the hunger in his spirit with the Word of God.

In April of 1995, Kathleen and I, along with our three young children, packed our bags and made the move to Croatia. I carried with me an English Bible, knowing how much it meant to Tihomir. He insisted on paying for it, but I had something better in mind for his payment. I told him that instead of money, his true offering would be to take me every morning to the mountains at 5:00 AM to pray.

That was the moment our journey together truly began.

From that day forward, we became inseparable. It wasn't just friendship—it was brotherhood, forged through prayer, through shared vision, through a relentless pursuit of bringing the love of Jesus to those who had yet to experience it. He became like family, a companion in faith who stood beside me through every hardship, every triumph, every battle we faced in the mission field.

Within months, Tihomir moved in with Kathleen and me, seamlessly blending into the rhythms of our home. He helped with our day-to-day responsibilities—assisting in the growing of a young church, supporting our family, and pouring himself into the work of ministry. He wasn't merely a helper or a disciple; he was a pillar, someone who carried the weight of the calling with us, never wavering in his dedication. He was gifted to speak English and translate for me, even when I teaching at the church we were pastoring.

Words fail to truly capture the depth of our bond. It was as though our souls had been intertwined for a greater purpose, bound together by the Spirit of God in a love that mirrored that of David and Jonathan. It was the kind of devotion that made one willing to lay down everything, to sacrifice, to fight for one another—not out of obligation, but out of love, out of divine purpose.

Perhaps it was like the way Jesus loved John, His disciple—pure, unwavering, rooted in a shared mission to bring salvation to the world. That was the heart of our connection. We didn't simply serve God together—we carried each other through the calling, through the weight of responsibility, through the joys and sorrows alike.

That season, though filled with struggles, was one of the most beautiful of my life. To walk alongside someone so devoted, so transformed by the love of God, was a privilege I will forever treasure. The journey had begun, and together, we stepped forward—determined, unshaken, and bound by the unrelenting love of Christ.

Tihomir carried wounds far deeper than what anyone could see on the surface. His past was marred by pain, by brokenness, by experiences no child should have to endure. He once shared with me that his father had an affair, and his mother—unable to bear the heartbreak—had taken her own life. At just seven years old, he found himself exposed to things his young mind could not understand—images that would linger in the depths of his memory long after he first saw them.

Becoming a believer didn't erase the battles he faced. Instead, it brought them into the light, where he had to confront them. One of the hardest struggles he carried was dismissing intrusive thoughts and the visual remnants of his childhood exposure to pornography. It wasn't just a temptation—it was an imprint, something that had rooted itself in his mind long before he knew who Jesus was.

We had many difficult conversations about it. At that time, I didn't fully grasp the weight of the battle he was fighting. Having never been exposed to pornography myself, I could not understand its grip, the way it manipulated the mind and fought to keep a person captive. Now, as a therapist working with men and women facing this very struggle, I see it with clarity—the stronghold it creates, the way it distorts relationships, the quiet shame it buries deep within the soul.

Back then, my solution was simple: "pray. Just stop thinking about it. Move forward." I had no knowledge, skills or experience in understanding addictions and childhood abuse. What I didn't realize was that the enemy does not retreat easily—especially not when someone is committed to serving the Lord. The stronger Tihomir became in his faith, the more relentless the battle was. And though I couldn't fully understand, I refused to abandon him in his struggle.

Our relationship was widely known in town. Tihomir came from wealth, studying to be a lawyer, surrounded by privilege and status. He moved in circles of affluence, frequenting places where only the elite were welcomed. He would take me to student restaurants where the rich children sat in the carpeted areas, indulging in elaborate meals, while those with less wealth were seated separately. The division was clear, the discrimination blatant.

Racism was deeply ingrained in the culture, and I faced it head-on. Some children, unfamiliar with my brown skin, would rub their fingers against my arm, expecting the colour to smear away like paint. They didn't understand, and in their ignorance, they mocked. But what mattered was that Tihomir never wavered.

In the middle of those restaurants, in the heart of the marketplace—where whispers spread and judgment lingered—he would look at me and say, "Pastor, can I give you a hug?" And he would embrace me.

Not like a casual friend, not with hesitation or restraint, but with the warmth of a brother reunited after years apart. As if I were his own flesh and blood, someone he refused to let go.

In those moments, love defeated every prejudice, every doubt, every expectation that the world had placed upon us. He did not care about the opinions of others, the rumors, the judgment. He saw me for who I was, and he chose, time and time again, to stand with me.

We had our battles. We had our differences. But at the core of it all was something unshakable—grace. A grace that covered his struggles. A grace that strengthened our bond. A grace that reminded us both that no matter what we faced, no matter the wounds that tried to hold us back, the love of God was greater. And that love was what carried us forward.

There are moments in life when love is so undeniable, so pure, that it defies reason. Tihomir embodied that kind of love—the kind that asked for nothing in return yet gave everything.

I remember the day I casually mentioned craving McDonald's. I wasn't expecting anything to come of it; it was just a passing thought. But Tihomir, in his relentless kindness, decided that no craving of mine would go unanswered. He drove seven hours—across borders, through unfamiliar roads—all to buy me a burger, went all the way to Italy.

He was the first person in my life who suggested to have dinner to celebrate the goodness of God in his life. He was grateful for being able to live with Kathleen and I, the friendship we developed and the times we had together in the presence of God, those prayer times at 5am. He selected a fancy restaurant, Italian food. Today when I think of Italian food, I have intrusive thoughts of him and the memory when we celebrated friendship.

When we finally sat down after a bit of wait time, he didn't just order food; he ordered two entire pizzas, ensuring that we shared something greater than just a meal—fellowship, laughter, warmth. That night, as we ate, it was as if we had stepped out of the weight of war and into a small moment of peace, of joy, of normalcy. It was the most delicious pizza I had ever had—not because of the flavor but because of the heart behind it.

I had always been the one to offer, to pay for meals, to take care of others. That is my nature. But this time, someone cared for me, other than my wife. Someone made sure I felt seen, appreciated, valued—not just as a pastor, not just as a leader, but simply as a man, as a friend, as a brother.

The war made everything uncertain, but one thing that never wavered was Tihomir's presence. On long drives through hostile territory, he would stop the car in the middle of nowhere and suggest we spend time in prayer. And there, surrounded by nothing but the wilderness, we would stand before God for thirty minutes, lifting our voices, surrendering our fears. Those were sacred moments—ones that carried the weight of eternity, ones I will hold onto forever.

He was there when our landlord, upon discovering that we were not Catholics, threw us out in the middle of the night. Three young children in tow, nowhere to go, nowhere to sleep. It was cruel, it was reckless, it was heartbreaking. And yet, Tihomir stood by us, unwavering, refusing to let us face that moment alone. He even endured violence for protecting us, roughed up for not disclosing our faith sooner. But it didn't matter to him. What mattered was that we were safe, that we had hope, that we didn't feel abandoned.

He was there when we found shelter at a church member tiny one-bedroom home, only to be threatened again. A Catholic priest warned the landlord that if we didn't leave, the house would be blown apart with bomb threats. Forced to move again, to run to search—Tihomir stood beside us through it all, fighting for a place where we could simply exist.

He was there when we had nowhere to go, when we found ourselves stuck at a train station, sleeping on the ground. He watched over us as Kathleen and I took turns through the night—me as a mattress for the children, Kathleen keeping guard, Tihomir tirelessly searching for a place for us to stay. He carried the weight of our burdens as if they were his own, never hesitating, never questioning.

He was there when hatred turned physical, when stones were thrown at us, when threats of soldiers coming to kill us became terrifyingly real as advised by a Catholic priest. My picture sat on a priest's desk, and when I met with him, he labeled me "as a wolf in sheep's clothing." My family was in danger, our mission to support people, plant a Bible college were attacked. And yet, even in the face of such hostility, Tihomir never left.

He was there for every trial, every victory, every heartbreak. And then, one day, he was gone.

It was a tragic accident. A moment that shook the church, the community, his family, his friends. The pain was unbearable, made worse by the whispers, the blame that found its way to me. They said it was my fault. They needed someone to carry the weight of grief, of anger, of injustice, and somehow, I became the target.

But Tihomir was never a victim—he was a warrior. He was a man who loved deeply, who gave selflessly, who walked fearlessly in his faith. He was my angel, my brother, my greatest gift in the midst of the storm.

And if given the chance, I would do it all again.

Not because the pain wasn't real. Not because I wouldn't change some things. But because love—pure, unwavering, relentless love—is worth every sacrifice.

And Tihomir's love, the love we shared in Christ, is something that will never fade, never be forgotten. It endures, always.

It was a Monday evening, just like any other, yet unknowingly, it would be the night that changed everything.

Tihomir and I had planned to visit his father's beach house for prayer, something we often did to retreat into the presence of God and find peace in the midst of war and uncertainty. He had been drafted as a soldier, and the weight of that reality rested heavily upon him. He was battling not only the looming dangers of war but also the deeply ingrained struggles of his past—intrusive thoughts from childhood exposure to pornography, the pain of his father's decisions being upset that he had become a born-again believer, and the recent financial strain of his broken-down car costing over $7000 German marks to fix.

Still, despite his burdens, he was a man of deep faith, unwavering in his commitment to seek God.

The Friday before his death, we sat together by the beach as the sun painted the sky in hues of gold and crimson. There was something different in the way he spoke, as though he knew—deep down—that his time on earth was nearing its end. He asked me to promise him one thing: that I would tell his family about Jesus, that I would share with them the transformation that had taken place in his life. It was a request that felt heavier than any conversation we had ever had, though at the time, I didn't realize just how prophetic his words were.

Sunday evening came, and with it, an unshakable burden for my friend. I could feel it pressing upon me, weighing down my spirit. I walked to the pier where we often met to pray and intercede for the people in our lives. That evening, I prayed for him with everything in me, sensing his depression and the battle he was fighting internally. And as I poured my heart out, I felt a strange peace—a reassurance that somehow, everything was going to be okay.

And then Monday arrived. We had planned to meet at his father's beach house, a quiet place about forty minutes outside the city. When I saw him earlier in the day, he had my coat on, and I wore his—an exchange so simple, so unremarkable, yet one that would soon become painfully significant. He had the keys to the beach house. He drove, and I took the bus, arriving just minutes after him.

What I didn't know—what I couldn't have imagined—was that in those few moments, everything had already unraveled.

As he stood there, watching the sunset—the very same sight we had admired together just days before—a truck hit him.

It took his life instantly.

I arrived at the beach house, waiting for him, never suspecting that just a stone's throw away, my best friend was lying on the pavement, gone from this world.

That night, an unbearable weight filled the air. A tightness gripped my chest, an invisible force choking me as I prayed, as I pleaded with God to bring him safely to me. But he never came.

The next morning, the truth crashed into me like a tidal wave. I called our church secretary, expecting her to tell me he had gotten delayed, expecting to hear that everything was fine. But her voice was cold, devoid of comfort.

"Tihomir is dead. And it's all your fault."

I couldn't comprehend it. I thought it was some cruel joke, some misunderstanding. But she was serious—deadly serious.

His family, grief-stricken and searching for something, someone, to blame, had placed the weight of his death on me. When they heard the accident had happened during the time of our scheduled prayer, they accused me of being part of a cult, of leading him into something that had ultimately ended his life.

The blame was suffocating.

I had to see him. I had to confirm what felt impossible. I asked someone to take me to the mortuary using all the Croatian language I knew, and when I arrived, his father's car was there. They allowed me in being his pastor, granted me the painful privilege of looking upon my dear friend for the last time.

There he lay, cold, motionless, on a steel table.

It wasn't real. It couldn't be real.

I stood there, staring at him, trying to feel something—grief, anger, sorrow—but instead, I felt nothing.

I could not cry. I could not process. My mind refused to accept what my eyes were seeing.

I reached out to a police friend for help, hoping to understand why this was happening, why his family had turned against me so quickly. He confirmed my worst fears—that they truly believed we were a cult, that they had decided it was our daily prayer that had killed him.

I was forbidden from attending his funeral. My police friend told me outright that if I went, Tihomir's community, his family, his friends—would kill me.

So Kathleen and several church members went in my place. They traveled to a small town called Imotski, where he was laid to rest, where the grief hung in the air like a fog too thick to see through.

And I was left behind, carrying the weight of it all. Carrying the pain. Carrying the blame. Carrying the loss of a man who had been my brother in every way that mattered. A man who, had it been me instead, would have never turned his back on me.

That day, I lost more than a friend. I lost a piece of my heart, a piece of my faith, a piece of myself.

And still, I would do it all again.

Because love—even in the midst of sorrow—is always worth it.

It took over twenty-six years before I finally returned to that little town, before I allowed myself to step into the place where the loss had first settled into my bones. By then, time had reshaped my grief, had dulled the sharp edges of pain, but the wound remained—silent, heavy, unspoken.

I traveled with my son Jadon and a member of the church in Croatia, determined to find Tihomir's grave, hoping that seeing it would bring the closure my soul had long searched for. We wandered through the cemetery, past stone markers etched with his last name, yet none of them belonged to him. Disappointment seeped in, but as I returned to the car, my son's voice cut through my thoughts.

"Dad, you know he's not there. Go and make your peace."

It was a truth I had known all along. His body may have been buried somewhere beneath the earth, but his spirit, his love, his laughter—all of it had long since transcended this world. Still, I needed to speak, to release the weight I had carried for so long.

So, I went back.

The cemetery was steeped in darkness, illuminated only by scattered candles flickering like whispers of remembrance. In one corner, a lone lamppost cast a pool of light, as if inviting me to stand there, to let everything out.

And I did. I spoke my anger. My frustration. My sorrow. I let the words pour out—toward God, toward Tihomir, toward the years that had slipped by without him.

And then, just as suddenly as the grief had swelled, peace washed over me. It wasn't dramatic, wasn't marked by any grand revelation. It was quiet, gentle, settling into the deepest parts of me where the pain had once lived.

AS FOR ME AND MY SPOUSE WE WILL PRAISE THE LORD

I was facing my reality. And in the midst of it all—in a silent cemetery, surrounded by nothing but candlelight and shadows—I felt no fear.

The church bells rang in the distance, their chime drifting through the cold air, and just beyond the lamppost, I noticed a young man walking, his silhouette framed by the glow.

Something about it felt significant, though I couldn't place why.

I left the cemetery, stepped into the car, and felt a weight I hadn't realized I'd still been carrying lift from my shoulders.

For twenty-six years, I had never ceased to praise the Lord. Kathleen and I had continued in ministry, had never allowed grief to steal the calling placed upon our lives. As I had learned to compartmentalize the pain, to tuck it away in the corners of my heart, somewhere in my mind that I refused to examine too closely.

I had barely allowed myself to look at his photos, and when I did—when his face stared back at me—I broke.

Every memory came rushing in, drowning me in the life we had lived together, the laughter we had shared, the purpose we had carried.

There were nights when Kathleen and I cried together, when we let ourselves remember him, when we relived the moments that had shaped our time in Croatia. Kathleen and I sat together, hands entwined, lifting our voices in worship. It was in moments like these that we felt most alive—most connected to the strength that had carried us through battles seen and unseen. Praise had always been our refuge, our fortress, the place where fear had no power.

As we sang along to Steven Curtis Chapman's *When You Are a Soldier*, the words seemed to echo the very heartbeat of our journey. Every verse, every melody felt like a reflection of the promises we had made to each other, of the battles we had faced side by side.

"When you are a soldier, I will be your shield. I will go with you into the battlefield."

Those words spoke to the deepest parts of our love, a reminder that we had never fought alone. When life threw arrows of doubt, when circumstances tried to wound us, we held on to each other, held on to the unwavering presence of God.

Kathleen had been my shield, just as I had been hers. There were times when exhaustion threatened to wear us down, when the weight of ministry, of family, of loss felt too heavy. But we never let go. Worship became the lifeline, the anchor that kept us moving forward when strength was all but gone.

"When you're tired from running, I will cheer you on. Look beside you and you'll see you're not alone."

There were moments of weeping, moments of uncertainty, yet never moments of abandonment. When I struggled, Kathleen carried me with her prayers. When she faltered, I reminded her of the unshaken promises of God. And when both of us felt weak, praise lifted us up.

"I will be the one you can cry your songs to. My eyes will share your tears. And I'll be your friend if you win or if you're defeated."

Victory and defeat had danced closely throughout our lives. We had stood in triumph and we had knelt in brokenness. But in all things, our love remained steadfast, rooted not only in each other but in the presence of the One who had called us.

We had seen dark days—days when loss whispered that we could not go on, days when fear tried to consume our faith. Yet worship had always been the light, guiding us out, reminding us of who we were, who He was, and the power of His grace.

"When you're lost in darkness, I will hold the light. I will help you find your way through the night."

AS FOR ME AND MY SPOUSE WE WILL PRAISE THE LORD

Even now, years later, when we sit in the quiet and reflect on the battles we've endured, the love of God still surrounds us. We never stopped singing. We never stopped lifting our hands in surrender. And through every valley, every hardship, we have kept the flame alive.

I look at Kathleen, and I know—we have been soldiers in faith. We have fought with praise, we have marched with worship, and we have stood victorious because of the One who never let us go.

And as long as we have breath, we will keep singing. Because worship is our shield. Because praise is our strength. Because the battlefield belongs to the Lord. And He has already won.

But even now, even knowing the final outcome—knowing the pain, the loss, the unbearable grief—the answer remained the same.

Yes. I would do it again.

A thousand times over, I would go. I would step into the unknown. I would give everything I had to bring people to the knowledge of the truth—that Jesus loves them, that He died for them, that His grace reaches further than any sorrow could ever touch.

Because God does send angels.

Some people come into our lives for a season, to strengthen us, to push us toward the destiny He has designed for us.

I don't know why Tihomir had to die, and perhaps I never will.

But I believe this—I believe that when we are vulnerable, the enemy tries harder, fights more viciously, seeks to destroy what is good.

And that is why we must remain covered, must keep the armor of God wrapped around us, must soak our lives in prayer, in praise, in worship.

Because only in His presence can we truly stand against the darkness.

And only in His presence can we find the strength to keep moving forward.

Through everything Kathleen and I endured—the heartbreak, the loss, the uncertainty—one truth became undeniable: there is power in praise, and God's presence manifests in worship.

We had built our marriage, our ministry, our very existence on this foundation. And because of it, we found the strength to move forward. No amount of regret, sorrow, or longing could rewrite the past, but the present remained in our hands—something we could shape, something we could pour into, something we could make beautiful for the future.

It was this understanding that led me to pursue psychology. I needed to grasp more than just spiritual principles; I wanted to comprehend the deeper workings of the human mind, the behaviors that drive us, the struggles that ensnare us. I wanted to understand addiction, mental health, diagnoses—the science behind suffering.

Because I had seen it firsthand.

I had watched people wrestle with inner battles they could not name, had seen faith collide with the complexities of trauma. I had walked beside those who struggled to break free from patterns of destruction, unable to reconcile their desires with their pain. And I had witnessed the way worship could reach places that words, therapy, and even logic could not touch.

Kathleen and I had learned, through the years of unexpected struggles and situations we could not have prepared for, that praise develops strength. Worship builds stamina. It creates stability in places where fear and doubt threaten to shake the foundation.

It was the very thing that carried us.

And it is the very thing that will continue to carry us—no matter what lies ahead.

IN THE FACE OF FEAR

That night in Croatia, at four in the morning, fear gripped my heart like never before. Kathleen and I had settled into the routine of our mission work in Split, Croatia, ministering to the young people in the city, living out God's calling despite the unpredictable dangers surrounding us. We had grown accustomed to hearing bombs behind the mountains in Split, where we lived, and had learned to sleep through the uncertainty. But nothing prepared us for the sound of gunfire directly in front of our home.

Earlier that evening, I had been in the city, evangelizing as I did every night. It had become a rhythm, meeting with young people, sharing the gospel, and witnessing lives being transformed by God's power. On this particular night, over twenty-three young men had gathered around me, their concern palpable. I was the only Indian brown man in the city during that time, aside from the foreign soldiers who passed through occasionally. Word had spread that skinheads were planning to kill me, and the young men insisted on escorting me home, ensuring my protection. Twelve of them rode the bus with me, standing guard until I reached my door. Their loyalty and care reminded me of how the early church must have felt, standing together in unity amidst persecution, guarding one another through prayer and presence.

As Kathleen and I settled into bed, we did what we always did—closed the steel blinds, prayed for peace, and committed the night into God's hands. But hours later, the sharp crack of gunfire shattered the silence. My heart nearly leaped out of my chest as terror overwhelmed me. Were they attacking our home? Had the warning about the skinheads come true? Were we moments away from dying?

I could hardly breathe as the gunfire continued. Though it lasted only a minute or two, it felt like an eternity. My mind raced, thinking about Kathleen, about our three small children sleeping just rooms away. I wanted to run, to take them to safety, but there was nowhere to go. The bomb shelter was five kilometers away, and unless the city siren blared, we had to remain inside.

At that moment, something miraculous happened. Instead of cries of fear, praise began to pour from my lips. Worship filled our home, not out of forced obedience, but out of raw desperation. Kathleen joined me, and together, we sang, prayed, and thanked God that no bullets had entered our home. Praise and worship were no longer just a part of our mission—it was our survival.

It reminded me of Paul and Silas in Acts 16, sitting in a prison cell, beaten and chained, yet choosing to lift their voices in praise. The chains did not dictate their faith; their worship dictated their freedom. And as they sang, God moved—the prison shook, the doors flung open, and their captivity was broken. That night in Croatia, as fear threatened to strangle me, praise became our weapon. Though the soldiers kept moving, though the war was far from over, our spirits found victory through worship. We were not just singing to ease our worry—we were declaring that fear had no hold over us.

Praise and worship carried us through more than just that terrifying night. It sustained us through years of uncertainty, through the mission field in a war-torn country, through raising seven children, through financial struggles, through moments when faith was tested beyond measure. Worship became the foundation that kept us from collapsing under the weight of responsibility.

Time and again, I saw in Scripture how worship was not just an act—it was a weapon. When Jehoshaphat faced an overwhelming army in 2 Chronicles 20, he did not send warriors ahead—he sent worshipers. And as they sang praises, God caused confusion among the enemy, and they turned on one another until Judah's victory was assured. Worship did what weapons could not. Worship fought battles we could never win on our own.

Kathleen and I had faced countless challenges throughout our ministry, but every time praise and worship were present, fear lost its grip. Whether in Croatia, in parenting, or in trusting God for financial provision, praise became our pathway to peace. When we focused on God's greatness rather than our circumstances, anxiety melted away.

That night in Croatia, our foundation of praise and worship were tested. It could have been a moment of collapse—where fear dictated our decisions, where panic led us into despair. But worship held us together. It reminded us that no battle was too great for God, that no amount of darkness could overshadow the light of His presence.

Praise and worship do not remove the trials; they transform how we walk through them. It is easy to worship when blessings abound, but it is in the moments of crisis that worship becomes a true lifeline. Kathleen and I have seen this truth unfold in every chapter of our journey. And as we continue to build our lives upon praise, we know that no matter what comes, God remains faithful. Fear does not get the final word—worship does.

That night in Croatia marked a turning point—not just in our ministry, but in our understanding of the supernatural presence of God. We had already witnessed His faithfulness in incredible ways, but this was something different. It was as though heaven had opened above us, and the atmosphere became so thick with His glory that anyone who

IN THE FACE OF FEAR

stepped into it felt an undeniable force. Some described it as a weight so heavy yet comforting, as if God Himself was pressing down upon the earth, making His presence known. Others said it felt like electricity in the air, a tangible energy that could be felt in the depths of their being.

It began with worship. Kathleen and I had committed to praise, even when fear knocked at the door, even when uncertainty clouded our path. The presence of God grew stronger each time we gathered, each time we lifted His name, until the evidence of His power was undeniable. In church services, people would fall under the power of God—not because of hype or emotionalism, but because His presence was so overwhelming that their bodies could no longer stand under it. Some wept uncontrollably, others laughed with indescribable joy, and many simply collapsed, encountering the Lord in a way they had never known.

Perhaps the greatest miracle of all was when I began playing the keyboard and singing in Croatian—without ever having learned the instrument or spoken the language fluently. The Holy Spirit moved through me, guiding my fingers across the keys, placing words on my lips that resonated with the people we were ministering to. In moments of worship, I wasn't thinking—I was simply responding to the presence that had overtaken me.

Before I knew it in a few months, I had written ten songs, all in Croatian, and in the dialect of Split, all carrying the message of revival and hope. When the producer who worked with the prime minister of Croatia heard about our worship, he reached out, and those songs became an album, titled *Rise Up, Croatia*. God had not only anointed the music—He had ordained its reach.

Then came the moment that stunned even the most skeptical hearts. On one of the islands during an all-night prayer meeting, soldiers standing at a distance saw fire above our tent. They rushed toward us, convinced that something had caught ablaze. But as they stepped inside, there was no fire—only worship. The realization struck them, and one by one, they fell to their knees, surrendering their lives to Jesus. They had seen something that defied logic, something that could not be explained except by divine power.

Another unforgettable moment happened on the rocky beach where we planned a water baptism. About seventy people gathered, ready to publicly declare their faith. As we worshiped, God's presence became so intense that people began to collapse onto the stones, overcome by His power. Some struggled to stand, others were lifted in prayer, and all felt the unmistakable nearness of God. It wasn't just an emotional experience—it was an encounter with the Almighty.

But not everyone understood. Spectators watching from a distance accused us of putting people into a trance. Suspicion grew, and they called the police, convinced that something unnatural was happening. When the officers arrived, we explained who we were, why we were there, and what we hoped to bring to the people—a message of hope, love, and faith. Though initially cautious, the police officers acknowledged that we were helping their people, offering prayer, kindness, and support in ways that truly mattered. They allowed us to continue our ministry, seeing no harm in what we were doing.

Through every moment, through every instance where God's presence overshadowed us, one truth became undeniable—God honours faithfulness. When we refuse to bow to fear, when we choose praise over panic, when we make worship our foundation, His presence flows freely. Kathleen and I had seen revival unfold, not because of anything we had done, but because we had remained obedient to the call. Praise was our strength, and worship was our weapon. The presence of God was not something we sought—it was something that found us because we never gave up.

The transformation of the police officer in Croatia was a moment Kathleen and I could never have predicted, yet looking back, it was evident that God had been preparing his heart all along. His curiosity was undeniable. For years, he had been watching us, observing how we lived, how we carried ourselves, and how the young people spoke about our work. We did not know at the time that he was silently questioning, wrestling with the contrast between his world and ours.

It all started at the police station, where he processed visas for foreigners. One day, he called for me to visit him. Walking into the building, I saw a line of over fifty people waiting for their documents, yet when I arrived, he ignored the queue and invited me into his office. He offered me something to drink and settled in as though he had nothing else to do but speak with me. It struck me—this man, whose job was to enforce regulations, who likely had seen foreigners come and go without a second thought, was giving me his full attention.

His question was simple but profound. Why had I, an outsider with no Croatian heritage, brought my wife and three small children into a country ravaged by war? Why would we risk everything for a people we did not know? His disbelief was tangible. In his mind, there had to be another motive, something that made sense because pure selflessness did not fit into his understanding of the world. I told him the truth—the story of the gospel, the mission of Jesus, and the call found in the book of Acts to go into all the world and make disciples. He listened, but I could tell he struggled to believe me. He met with me occasionally, asking more questions, as if trying to catch me in an inconsistency. But there was nothing to hide.

After the war ended and Kathleen and I returned to Canada, I continued visiting Croatia every few months. One visit changed everything. The officer invited me to his home, where his mother had prepared lunch for us. The warmth of the meal, the simplicity of the gathering—it felt like a turning point. After eating, he led me to his bedroom, where he displayed a collection of guns, bullets, and military artifacts. The sight made me uneasy. I wondered where this conversation was headed, whether he was revealing something deeper, maybe even testing me. Then, in the middle of that room filled with weapons, he asked the question that would shift his life forever.

"I want to ask you something," he said. "I have been watching you for over three years. You are always smiling. You are always full of joy. The young people call you 'the black pope.' Some people say you have been putting people into a trance. I have heard about how you have been feeding the hungry with shipments of food from Lester Sumrall. I want what you have. I want your Jesus."

At that moment, time seemed to pause. All his skepticism, all his questioning—it had led him here, to this moment of surrender. Sitting on his bed, he repeated the sinner's prayer after me. And as he spoke the words, his voice shook, his eyes welled with tears, and suddenly, the house began to tremble. His mother, still in the kitchen, called out, asking, "What are you boys doing? The house is shaking."

But we were not doing anything. It was God.

The presence of God came down so powerfully that even the walls could not contain it. This hardened officer, this man who had lived through war, who had carried weapons and enforced laws, was now weeping under the weight of God's love. He had spent years searching, testing, doubting, but in this moment, he could no longer deny the truth. Jesus was real.

That night, we stayed up past two in the morning reading the Bible together. He kept shaking his head, saying, "I cannot believe Jesus is so real." He wasn't just reading words on a page—he was encountering the living presence of God, one revelation at a time.

The next step came naturally to him. He asked to be baptized, even though it was the middle of winter. The cold did not matter—he wanted to take this step without hesitation. When he emerged from the water, he grabbed onto me with such joy that it felt like he had won the greatest prize of his life. And he had.

IN THE FACE OF FEAR

Kathleen and I had never wavered in our praise, even when fear threatened to consume us, even when doubts arose. This was why. The power of praise and worship, the presence of God—it transforms even the most unlikely hearts. We had seen soldiers fall to their knees, we had seen people collapsing under the weight of God's glory, but this officer was different. He had spent years doubting, yet in a single encounter, his entire life was rewritten.

This is what praise does. It makes space for God to move, to enter the deepest crevices of the human heart, to bring life where there was once only skepticism. Worship is not just a song—it is an invitation for heaven to touch earth. And as Kathleen and I watched this man, once filled with doubts, now consumed by joy, we knew we would never stop praising the Lord.

The journey of faith is rarely a straight path, and often, God moves in ways we don't fully comprehend until much later. As Kathleen and I lived and served in Croatia, we saw firsthand how His presence surrounded us, how praise and worship became more than just spiritual practices—they became our refuge, our guide, and our shield. That became especially clear in moments like the incident on the train, where injustice struck, but God's hand was already working behind the scenes.

Another incident when praise and worship was ushered to God. It all started with the passport theft, a frustrating but necessary detour that led my friend Tihomir and me on an unexpected trip to Zagreb, the capital of Croatia. With no other option but to visit the Canadian Embassy, we set out, unaware that this journey would become a defining moment. The snowstorm that swept in as we traveled was intense, and it was no surprise when Tihomir's car lost traction, sliding down a hill and leaving us stranded. The only solution was to transport the car by train back to Split, as it was no longer driveable—a complication that only added to the mounting stress.

Yet, even in this moment of uncertainty, God was orchestrating connections that would later prove vital. On the train back, Tihomir bought me a cup of coffee, a simple act of kindness, but one that did not go unnoticed. I heard the voices of two police officers making a comment they did not expect me to understand: *"Why are you buying coffee for the black man?"* Their words carried weight, not only because of the ignorance they reflected but because of what followed.

I mentioned their words to my friend, and soon after, the train's server relayed the message to the officers of what I had said. What happened next was something I could have never imagined. My friend was taken into a separate room, where these officers—apparently intoxicated—brutally assaulted him. The injuries were severe—his kidney bruised, his eardrum cracked. It was senseless violence, fueled by prejudice and abuse of power. And in that moment, all we could do was pray.

This was the kind of injustice that could make anyone question their purpose, their mission, and their faith. Why had this happened? Why was my friend suffering for something so trivial as buying coffee for me? But this was also where praise and worship took on their most profound role. We had learned that worship was not just about celebrating when things were good—it was about trusting when things were unclear. So even as we wrestled with anger, frustration, and confusion, we did the only thing we knew to do. We praise God with our worship. And while we did not understand in that moment why this had happened; God was already working on our behalf.

The police officer who had given his life to Jesus—the same man who had watched me for years, who had doubted, questioned, and tested my faith—was about to be instrumental in bringing justice. He worked with me and Tihomir to file a disciplinary report against the officers responsible for the attack. The result was swift. They were suspended, their reckless actions exposed. Apparently, their drunkenness had

IN THE FACE OF FEAR

contributed to their aggression that night, but that did not excuse what had been done. Justice was served.

I often reflect on that moment—not just the pain of it, but the way God had positioned people exactly where they needed to be. If that police officer had never encountered a desire to know me and the love of God, if his heart had never been transformed, would we have had someone willing to fight for justice on our behalf? Would things have unfolded differently? It is impossible to say for sure, but one thing is clear—God was already working before we even knew we needed Him to.

Kathleen and I have learned that praise and worship do not merely lift spirits; they invite divine intervention. They prepare the way for encounters, for protection, for breakthrough—even in situations that seem unfair or unbearable. This experience was proof that no matter what happens, God is still moving, still connecting the right people at the right time, still ensuring that His purposes are fulfilled. We may never fully understand *why* certain things happen, but we do know that when we stand firm in worship, God never fails to reveal His greater plan.

And in the end, even through pain, even through confusion, our hearts remained full of praise. Because what the enemy had meant for harm, God turned for good. And that is why we worship—not just in joy, but in trust, knowing that He is always, always working.

THE PRELUDE TO PASSION

Setting the stage for praise in a marriage is essential—it is the foundation that strengthens love, deepens faith, and creates a sacred space for God's presence to dwell. Some couples find it difficult to praise God side by side, hesitating to open their hearts fully in front of each other. Perhaps it is pride, fear, or simply unfamiliarity with shared spiritual intimacy. But when love is true, nothing should stand between two people—not embarrassment, not hesitation. And if God is at the center, then worship must flow freely, unhindered by proximity, unhindered by self-consciousness.

Kathleen and I have embraced praise as a vital part of our marriage, it is our prelude to passion. We don't reserve it for church alone—it fills the spaces in our everyday lives. Whether we're driving, sitting in the living room, or standing before God in a service, praise is our refuge. There is something profound about standing together in His presence, hands raised, hearts surrendered. Sometimes, I glance at Kathleen as she praise, and in those moments, I love God even more—because He gave me the perfect partner, a woman who loves Him first and loves me completely.

Holding hands as we praise the Lord and worship Him, tears streaming down our cheeks as the presence of God surrounds us—there is no greater joy. Praise is what binds us together, what lifts us beyond life's burdens, what ensures that no matter the storms, we remain anchored in Him.

Even in the ordinary moments, praise is present. While cooking, washing dishes, or simply going about the day, I can hear Kathleen's voice somewhere in the house, lifting songs of praise to the Lord. Sometimes, as I play the piano, she is moving around, caught in the rhythm of praise that flows naturally through our home.

Morning devotions set the tone for the day—first in personal reflection, then together as we join hands, lifting our voices in praise before stepping into the responsibilities ahead. At night, when life feels heavy, when stress tries to weigh us down, Kathleen and the children gather in prayer, and suddenly, songs of praise fill the air. It is in these moments that we remember— praise is not dependent on circumstance. We praise Him in the storms, and we praise Him in the sunshine.

Praise is not just an act confined to a specific moment in the day—it is the very atmosphere we cultivate in our homes, shaping our thoughts, interactions, and spiritual outlook. Setting the stage for praise in the home means establishing a foundation where God's presence is not merely acknowledged but actively invited into every aspect of daily life. This practice not only strengthens faith but also fosters peace, unity, and spiritual resilience, carrying its effects through every moment of the day.

Deuteronomy 6:4-9 emphasizes the importance of embedding God's truth in our hearts and homes. It commands us to love the Lord with all our heart, soul, and might, and to diligently teach His words to our children—speaking of them throughout daily activities. This is not a passive suggestion but an intentional directive to ensure that worship and devotion are seamlessly integrated into the fabric of life. When we rise in the morning, when we sit in our homes, when we go about our tasks, and even when we rest at night—God's presence should remain central.

Kathleen and I have understood this principle from the time we got married, making praise and worship the fragrance of our mornings. It is more than a routine; it is how we prepare our hearts for the day ahead, shaping the spiritual atmosphere in our home. When we start our day in praise, we are not just setting aside time for God—we are surrendering our emotions, concerns, and plans to Him. Praise aligns our hearts with His purpose, shielding us from distractions and setting the tone for how we interact with one another.

Scripture teaches us that praise satisfies three core human needs: the rational, volitional, and emotional. The mind longs for understanding, the will seeks direction, and the heart desires fulfillment. Praise answers all these needs. It provides truth that satisfies intellectual inquiry, commands that guide behaviour, and a relationship with God that brings deep joy. When praise is absent, these needs are often misdirected toward idols—materialism, self-reliance, or fleeting pleasures that fail to truly satisfy. But when praise is present, it anchors our souls in truth and restores balance to our spiritual lives.

The influence of praise extends beyond personal spirituality—it transforms relationships. Praise in the home prevent tension, misunderstandings, and disputes. Arguments that may have erupted due to stress or frustration are diffused when worship takes precedence. It is difficult to harbor resentment or anger when lifting up God's name, as worship invites a posture of humility, gratitude, and peace. The presence of God settles the home, ensuring that love and understanding take precedence over discord.

Additionally, praise shapes the faith of our children, teaching them to rely on God and seek His guidance in all aspects of life. As Deuteronomy states, parents are to instill God's truth diligently—speaking of Him in daily routines, making His presence a natural and familiar part of their children's lives. A home saturated in praise fosters spiritual maturity, allowing children to grow up with a strong foundation of faith, rather than merely learning about God on Sundays.

Carrying praise throughout the day requires intentionality. It means remaining mindful of God's presence in every situation—expressing gratitude during moments of joy, turning to Him in moments of struggle, and keeping His truth at the forefront of decision-making. Praise is not restricted to morning prayers; it is maintained through conversations, actions, and even quiet moments of reflection. Whether at home, at work, or in interactions with others, the peace cultivated through morning praise should extend outward, shaping attitudes and responses.

Many believers struggle with feeling disconnected from praise due to modern challenges—secular influences, distractions, and even dissatisfaction with church worship experiences. However, true praise transcends external circumstances. It is not dependent on church structures or emotional highs; it is a consistent practice of surrender and devotion. When praise becomes a daily rhythm, it strengthens spiritual resilience, ensuring that faith remains firm regardless of outside pressures.

Kathleen and I have seen firsthand how praise transforms the home, the heart, and the mind. It is not just an expression of faith; it is a way of life that keeps us grounded, joyful, and aligned with God's purpose. By setting the stage for worship each morning, we invite peace, unity, and divine guidance into our home, ensuring that His presence carries us through every part of the day.

We have always known that praise was more than a Sunday ritual. It was a way of life, a foundation upon which our marriage, our family, and our faith were built. From the earliest days of our relationship, we understood that praise was the keys to staying together. It was not just about singing songs or saying prayers—it was about cultivating an atmosphere of peace, unity, and divine presence in our home. Through worship, we found strength, clarity, and renewal, shaping our lives in ways that kept us grounded and connected.

Praise has always been our source of strength. When life brought challenges, when disagreements arose, or when uncertainty clouded our path, praise became the force that held everything together. Praise has a way of shifting perspectives. Instead of focusing on problems, it reminds us of God's sovereignty. Instead of dwelling on frustrations, it invites peace. Kathleen and I have experienced this firsthand, seeing how beginning our day with praise prevented arguments and fostered a spirit of understanding. Praise does not erase difficulties, but it changes how we approach them. It strengthens us with divine reassurance and fills our hearts with gratitude.

Scripture repeatedly affirms the significance of praise as both a command and a privilege. Revelation 4:9-11 and Revelation 5:2, 8-14 paint a breathtaking picture of heavenly praise, where the elders and angels bow in adoration before God, declaring His worthiness. This truth has shaped our understanding of praise—it is not an obligation but a response to who God is. He alone is worthy of our praise, and that realization anchors our worship in love rather than duty.

One of the most powerful lessons we learned was the importance of setting the stage for praise. Praise does not just happen; it is cultivated. In Deuteronomy 6:4-9, God commands His people to keep His words in their hearts, teaching them to their children, speaking of them at all times—when sitting at home, walking along the way, and rising in the morning. This passage deeply resonated with us. Praise was meant to be constant, not sporadic. It was meant to fill the home, to shape conversations, and to remain present even in mundane moments. We saw firsthand how making worship a priority in the morning set the tone for the entire day. It created an atmosphere of peace and reverence, ensuring that our interactions were rooted in love rather than irritation.

THE PRELUDE TO PASSION

Psalm 100:1 declares, "*Make a joyful noise unto the Lord, all ye lands.*" Praise is not meant to be passive—it is an active expression of our love and reverence for God. Kathleen and I embraced this in our home, ensuring that worship was not limited to quiet moments but included heartfelt expressions of praise. Whether singing aloud, reading scripture, or simply pausing to reflect on His goodness, we kept the presence of worship alive.

There is something deeply transformative about praising the Lord together as husband and wife. From a psychological perspective, praise influences emotions, rewires thought patterns, and reduces anxiety. Studies show that engaging in spiritual practices strengthens neural pathways associated with gratitude and emotional regulation. When we worship, we shift our focus from ourselves to God, breaking cycles of negativity and fostering resilience. Kathleen and I have witnessed how praise shapes attitudes, diffusing tension and realigning priorities. It has kept us connected, preventing minor disagreements from escalating, and ensuring that we approach each day with a spirit of humility and love.

The beauty of praise is that it manifests in different ways. We have always believed in praise through thanksgiving. Gratitude is a powerful act of praise —it shifts the heart toward joy and appreciation. Scripture repeatedly emphasizes the importance of giving thanks, showing that it is not just about acknowledging blessings but about aligning the heart with God's goodness. Deuteronomy 8:10 instructs, "*When you have eaten and are satisfied, praise the LORD your God for the good land he has given you.*" Giving thanks is not optional—it is foundational.

In Psalm 150, praise is described as a declaration of God's greatness, transcending circumstances and emotions. Kathleen instilled this truth in our family, reminding us that praise should be genuine, emerging from the heart rather than mere outward performance. When we praise, we affirm God's sovereignty, positioning ourselves in humility and trust. We sing after praying for our meals "Praise the Lord of Host for

His mercy endures forever." It is funny to hear others joining in how they mumble.

Giving is yet another act of praise, one that demonstrates faith and obedience. Scripture teaches that cheerful giving is a reflection of worship, recognizing that everything we have comes from God. Second Corinthians 9:6-8 reminds us that "God loves a cheerful giver."

Giving has been one of the most profound ways we have experienced the faithfulness of God. We have learned that no matter how much we pour out—whether time, talents, gifts, or finances—we can never outgive Him. Every act of obedience, every sacrifice, every moment spent in service has been met with His abundant blessings, proving again and again that He is faithful to those who trust Him.

God calls us to give sacrificially, just as Abel did in Genesis. Abel's offering was honoured because it was given with sincerity, with reverence, with a heart fully surrendered to God. We have embraced this principle within our family, making giving a natural part of our blueprint—not as an obligation, but as an overflow of worship.

It has been beautiful to see this heart of generosity take root in our children. Giving has never been something forced or demanded—it has been modeled, lived, and woven into our daily lives in a way that makes it second nature. They have given of themselves in mission trips, humanitarian efforts, and everyday moments, understanding that their resources—whether great or small—are meant to bless others and glorify God.

For us, giving is praise It is an acknowledgment of His provision, a declaration that all we have comes from Him. It is not about what we gain but about honoring Him with the very things He has entrusted to us. And in that surrender, we have found joy, favour, and the undeniable presence of His blessings surrounding our lives.

THE PRELUDE TO PASSION

Kathleen and I have always understood this principle, ensuring that our giving was done with joy and a spirit of trust. Whether through finances, time, or service, worship through giving allows us to live with open hands, acknowledging God's provision.

Praise through prayer and the Word has always been central in our lives. Prayer is our means of communication with God, aligning our hearts with His will and inviting His presence into our home. Luke 11:9 reminds us to persist in prayer, saying, " "So I say to you: Ask and it will be given to you; seek and you will find; knock and the door will be opened to you."

Praise through prayer keeps us connected with God, ensuring that our hearts remain aligned with His purpose. Scripture serves as the foundation upon which we build our faith, allowing His truth to shape our decisions and perspectives. Psalm 119:105 declares, " Your word is a lamp for my feet, a light on my path.," reminding us that praise also means seeking guidance in His Word.

One of the greatest acts of praise is obedience. Romans 12:1 reminds us that praise is not just about songs and rituals—it is about surrender, about offering our lives as a living sacrifice. We have taken this to heart, ensuring that our faith is not passive but active, demonstrated through the way we live and love.

The impact of praise goes beyond personal faith—it transforms relationships, it strengthens families, and it creates a foundation that withstands trials. Worship in our home is powerful. It is a safeguard against division, a remedy for chaos, and a source of unwavering peace. We have seen the difference when praise is present and when it is absent. Without it, the home becomes vulnerable to distractions and frustrations. But when worship is intentionally cultivated, the home becomes a sanctuary—a place where love, grace, and divine presence dwell.

AS FOR ME AND MY SPOUSE WE WILL PRAISE THE LORD

Carrying praise throughout the day is just as important as beginning with it. Praise should not be confined to morning prayers or evening reflections—it should be continuous, influencing responses, attitudes, and actions. Kathleen and I have ensured that praise remains active in our household, reminding one another to turn to God in all things. Whether in joyful moments or difficult situations, praise serves as our anchor, keeping us rooted in faith and purpose.

Praise has been the key to staying together. It has strengthened our marriage, shaped our family, and deepened our understanding of God. We have learned that praise is not just about expressing devotion—it is about experiencing transformation. It has filled our home with peace, guided us through uncertainty, and kept us connected to God and one another.

Every morning, every interaction, every moment is an opportunity to praise. Through praise, thanksgiving, prayer, and obedience, we ensure that our lives remain centered on Him. Praise is not just an act—it is the heartbeat of faith, the foundation of unity, and the source of unshakable strength. Kathleen and I will continue to embrace it, carrying its presence through every day and every season of life.

THE PRELUDE TO PASSION

SPARKS BEFORE THE FLAME

Kathleen and I started our journey together at a young age, stepping into marriage with little experience, knowledge, or understanding of what it truly meant to merge two lives. We were different in almost every way—she was quiet, thoughtful, and preferred to stay behind the scenes, while I thrived in the spotlight, engaging with people wherever I went. She was more introspective, I was more outspoken. We loved each other deeply, but those differences led to clashes, especially in the early years when we were learning how to navigate life together.

She was the first girl I had ever kissed with passion, the first person who made my heart race, who gave me butterflies in my stomach. Even today, after all these years, that feeling hasn't stopped. Yet, love alone was not enough to sustain our marriage—we needed something stronger, something that would anchor us when emotions flared, when frustrations boiled over, when life threw us challenges we weren't equipped to handle. That anchor, we learned, was praise and worship.

Early in our marriage, an opportunity came that tested our relationship. Out of more than a thousand applicants, I was selected for a prestigious leadership award to attend St. Bonaventure University in the United States. It was a huge honour, one that could shape my future in ways I had never imagined. But it also meant leaving Kathleen behind. The decision wasn't easy, and in the process of discussing it, arguments erupted. We fought over the uncertainty, the separation, the unknown challenges we would face with me being gone. Fear crept in—fear of change, fear of how distance would affect us, even thought it was for a short time.

I remember one night, after yet another heated discussion, we both sat in silence, exhausted from the debate. Then something shifted. Instead of continuing to argue, we decided to worship. We lifted our voices in prayer, thanking God for the opportunity, asking Him for clarity, and praising Him in advance for whatever His will would be. It wasn't instant, but as we surrendered the decision to God, peace flooded in. We knew then what we had to do—I would go. Though we still had fears, worship had reminded us that God was bigger than our concerns, that He was leading us.

Praise became my refuge in those moments of struggle—not just in decision-making, but in everyday trials. Whenever Kathleen and I had disagreements, I didn't stay in frustration. I would leave the house and go into the streets, looking for young people to talk to about Jesus. It reminded me of Jesus' reaction when He heard that John the Baptist had been killed—He didn't sink into despair. He went about doing good, healing the sick, preaching the gospel, spreading love. I wanted to follow that example. Instead of dwelling on negativity, I used worship and outreach to redirect my heart.

I became known in the city as "Moses selling a drug named Jesus," "Preacher Boy," "The Jesus Guy." People invited me to bars where I would share Jesus with them. The presence of God stayed with me because I refused to let arguments or setbacks shake my faith. Praise and worship kept my spirit steady, helping me navigate not just marriage, but every hardship that came our way.

There were difficult moments, especially when financial struggles weighed us down. Raising a family, making ends meet, managing responsibilities—it wasn't always easy. So I developed a habit to ensure that I never lost my focus. I used to set three alarms—one by my bed, one in the bathroom, and one in our spare bedroom—all scheduled for 2 a.m. They forced me to wake up, to turn them off, to leave my bed and enter my place of prayer. I cheated sleep in order to seek God, knowing that praise was what would sustain us and worship will bring the presence of God.

I became addicted to His presence. There were nights when the Holy Spirit entered the room so powerfully that I felt an unseen force push me against the wall, as if a mighty wind had blown through the house. Sometimes, with my eyes closed in worship, I would feel as though someone had suddenly turned on a bright light. God was meeting me in those moments, reminding me that every burden we carried was already handled in His hands.

Praise and worship became the foundation of our marriage—not just a practice, but a necessity. When we were angry at each other, when stress made it hard to communicate, worship softened our hearts. Instead of letting anger take control, we turned to God. Even when we had no money to buy food, when our bills seemed impossible to pay, God provided. We would open the mailbox to find cash enclosed in an envelope, sent by someone we didn't know. To this day, we never discovered who sent that money, but we knew exactly where it came from—God's faithfulness.

Through every storm, worship never failed us. It did not take away the difficulties, but it changed how we faced them. It reminded us that our marriage was more than just two people trying to make life work—it was a covenant, strengthened and sustained by God. Praise bound us together, creating a cord that tied our hearts in ways nothing else could.

Marriage is never easy. It requires effort, sacrifice, patience. But praise and worship ensured that instead of focusing on problems, we kept our eyes on the One who held our future. We may have been young and inexperienced when we started, but praise and worship gave us wisdom beyond our years. They taught us how to love each other deeply, how to move through hardship with faith, and how to trust that no matter what came, God would always be in control.

Kathleen and I had many reasons to quit, different cultures, upbringing, likes and dislikes, habits, behaviours, many moments where frustration could have led us away from our purpose. But worship kept us going. And because of that, love remained, faith grew, and our marriage became stronger than we ever imagined.

Life has a way of testing the heart, especially in moments when words cut deep and insecurities rise to the surface. We had always relied on praise and worship to guide us, to lift us in difficult times, but there are moments when pain tries to drown out the song in our hearts. That winter, when work slowed down and I sat at the dinner table with Kathleen's family, I experienced one of those moments.

Her uncle's words hit me harder than I could have anticipated. "You should have never gotten married if you know you will not work." It wasn't just a passing comment—it was a judgment, a wound that struck at the core of my identity. I had always worked hard, done my best to provide, yet in that moment, I felt reduced to nothing. The worst part wasn't just what was said—it was the silence. No one defended me. Not even Kathleen. I felt alone, as if my presence in the family had been a mistake, as if my worth had been questioned simply because circumstances weren't in my favour.

I walked away from that table, my thoughts spiraling, questioning everything. Should I leave? Should I distance myself? Was this what they truly thought of me? But as always, worship redirected my heart. Kathleen and I talked, and instead of letting bitterness take root, we turned to praise. We thanked God for His provision, even when the bank account was empty, even when others doubted, even when the future seemed uncertain. Worship reminded us that God, not man, was the one who determined our worth. And because of that, I was able to maintain my relationship with her family, to look beyond the hurt and embrace forgiveness.

But the enemy wasn't done testing my resolve. That same winter, when work finally came, I found myself standing on a scaffold in a massive, dark warehouse. It was so big it felt endless, stretching like a football field beneath me. The silence in that space echoed the doubts that had been planted in my mind. The negative words I had heard at dinner taunted me, replaying in my thoughts like a broken record. It was too much.

Standing nearly thirty to forty feet in the air, something inside me broke. Without fully thinking, I jumped.

In that split second, I wasn't sure what would happen. Would I hit the ground, break something, suffer an injury? Would this moment of despair define me? But as I fell, something unseen carried me. I was caught—not by human hands, not by chance, but by angels. Instead of crashing, I landed gently, unharmed, as though invisible arms had reached out and shielded me.

It was then that I understood how deep God's protection ran, how strong His presence was over my life. The praise I had sung day after day while working—the songs of worship that had filled that warehouse as I taped drywall—had not gone unheard. Heaven had been listening. And when I needed it most, heaven responded.

From that day forward, praise became even more vital in my life. It wasn't just an act—it was a weapon, a shield, a force that guarded me against despair. Even today, whether I'm at the gym, in my car, or walking outside, I worship. Because God has never ceased to be there for us. Kathleen and I have tapped into a power greater than words can fully explain—a power that sustains, protects, and strengthens, even in the darkest moments.

Marriage, in its purest form, is the intertwining of two lives, two histories, and often, two completely different perspectives. We knew from the beginning that our union was breaking new ground within our families. Ours was the first interracial marriage on both sides, which meant there were unspoken questions, quiet hesitations, and adjustments that needed to happen—not just between us, but among the people who loved us.

Kathleen's mother, though gentle in her approach, had suggested that perhaps it would be best if we remained just friends rather than pursuing something deeper. It wasn't out of cruelty or rejection, but likely out of concern—maybe for the unknown struggles that come with blending cultures, or perhaps for how others might perceive it. I never took it personally, but it was a reminder that love often faces resistance, even from well-meaning places.

For my family, things were different. They were not living in Canada when Kathleen and I started dating, so I kept our relationship to myself until the engagement. I didn't want to give space for doubt or interference. I had left home at eighteen, migrating to Canada on my own, and I had spent years navigating life independently. When I met Kathleen, I knew she was the one I wanted to build a life with, and I wasn't about to let fear or uncertainty stand in the way.

Still, moments came that tested our resilience. One Christmas, Kathleen's sister gave me a sweatshirt as a gift. At first, it seemed like a simple gesture—until I noticed the design. Nineteen white sheep and one black sheep. A little thing, maybe. But for me, it carried an unintended weight. The symbolism made my heart sink. My mind wandered to every connotation associated with being the "black sheep" of the family—the outsider, the odd one, the one who doesn't belong. I knew in my heart that Kathleen's sister loved me, that she had always been kind, that we had shared ministry together in street evangelism. Yet, in that moment, doubt whispered to me. Did she see me as

AS FOR ME AND MY SPOUSE WE WILL PRAISE THE LORD

different? Did her family truly accept me? Was I making a mistake in marrying into a world where I would always stand out?

For a brief time, I wrestled with these thoughts so intensely that I considered breaking off the engagement. The weight of doubt pressed on me, distorting truths, making me question what I knew in my spirit. But we turned to what had always sustained us—praise and worship. We sat together, singing Keith Green songs, trying to harmonize, losing ourselves in worship rather than fear. And as we worshiped, something remarkable happened. The presence of God filled the space between us, settling every anxious thought, dissolving every insecurity. Where doubt had crept in, peace overtook it. It was as if the Holy Spirit whispered, *You are exactly where you are meant to be.*

That moment changed everything. Praise became the bridge between human perception and divine truth. The sweatshirt was not an attack, nor was it a sign of rejection—it was simply a gift, given without the heavy meaning I had placed on it. Kathleen's sister and her husband remained our role models in building a strong family, and to this day, I see how their support was never absent, even when my thoughts tried to convince me otherwise.

Through praise, worship, and trust, Kathleen and I continued forward in our marriage, never allowing negativity to take root. We learned that love is not just about feelings—it is about faith, about choosing to see the best in each other and in those around us. And through it all, praise was our weapon, guarding our hearts, sealing our commitment, and ensuring that nothing—no fear, no doubt, no whispered insecurities—could break the bond God had formed between us.

SPARKS BEFORE THE FLAME

WHEN TWO HEARTS SING

Kathleen and I have discovered that praise and worship are not just expressions of faith—they are essential tools for keeping our relationship strong, navigating challenges, and standing firm against anything that threatens our unity. A couple that praises together stays together, because worship has the power to break tension, restore peace, and invite God's presence into every situation. Throughout Scripture, we see examples of how worship transformed circumstances, won battles, and strengthened relationships. We have experienced the same victories in our marriage as two hearts sing.

One of the clearest examples of worship winning battles is found in 2 Chronicles 20, when King Jehoshaphat faced a vast army that threatened to destroy Judah. Instead of panicking, he turned to God in prayer and instructed the people to praise. As the worshipers went ahead of the army, singing and lifting their voices to God, their enemies became confused and destroyed one another. Jehoshaphat and his people did not even have to fight—their praise brought victory.

Kathleen and I have seen how worship shifts our perspective in moments of tension. When disagreements arise, we have learned to pause and praise instead of arguing. In those moments, the presence of

God overtakes frustration, and suddenly, what seemed like a battle dissolves into peace.

When King Jehoshaphat faced overwhelming odds, Judah stood on the brink of destruction. A vast army had assembled against them, a force so great that by human standards, victory seemed impossible. Fear gripped the people, but instead of surrendering to despair, Jehoshaphat made a powerful decision—he turned to God. He did not organize his army for war, nor did he seek political alliances. Instead, he called the people of Judah to praise and worship.

Jehoshaphat declared a fast throughout Judah, leading the people in prayer. He stood before the assembly and acknowledged their dependence on God, confessing that they had no power against the approaching enemy. Then, God spoke through a prophet, delivering an astonishing command: Judah would not have to fight in this battle. The Lord Himself would take charge. Their only role? To stand firm, trust Him, and praise.

As the people worshiped, something extraordinary happened. When Judah's army marched out, they did not carry weapons—they carried songs of praise. The musicians and worshipers led the way, singing of God's faithfulness. And as they praised, confusion struck the enemy camp. The vast army that had assembled against Judah suddenly turned on itself. Instead of attacking Judah, the enemy forces fought each other. By the time Judah arrived, not a single enemy remained standing—the battle had been won without a single sword being lifted.

Kathleen and I have found that praise and worship hold this same power in relationships. Struggles arise, conflicts threaten unity, and sometimes, it feels like forces beyond our control are pushing love to its limits. But just as God used praise to dismantle Judah's enemies, worship can destroy every attack against a marriage.

There are moments when frustration builds, misunderstandings deepen, and the pressure of life feels overwhelming. The enemy thrives on division, resentment, and doubt. But when couples choose praise over panic, the enemy's plans unravel. We have learned that instead of allowing negativity to take root, we must disrupt it with worship. Worship invites God's presence into the relationship, and when He steps in, battles that seemed impossible are won effortlessly.

Just as the enemy forces in 2 Chronicles 20 fought against themselves, praise and worship cause chaos in the schemes of the enemy. The very things that were meant to destroy a relationship begin to collapse under their own weight. Instead of tearing couples apart, struggles lose their hold. Worship does not just strengthen a relationship—it dismantles every force trying to weaken it.

Praise shifts focus from the problem to the power of God. Kathleen and I have seen firsthand how worship replaces fear with confidence, anxiety with peace, and discord with unity. It is not about ignoring the struggles but about declaring that God is greater than them. Just as Judah stood firm in faith, couples must stand in worship, believing that God will bring resolution and renewal.

No battle is too great for God. Worship does more than lift spirits—it brings breakthrough. The enemies that once loomed large will crumble under the weight of praise. We continue to use worship as our greatest weapon, knowing that through it, no force can stand against the power of God.

Another powerful biblical example is Paul and Silas in Acts 16. After being unjustly imprisoned, they did not waste time complaining about their situation. Instead, they worshiped. As they sang hymns, the prison shook, the chains fell off, and their worship led not only to their freedom but to the salvation of the jailer and his family.

Kathleen and I have learned from this story that worship in difficult moments leads to breakthrough. When we feel overwhelmed by life's struggles—whether financial concerns, emotional burdens, or decisions we are unsure about—we lift our voices in praise. Worship reminds us that God is in control, and through it, we find clarity and solutions that were not apparent before.

Paul and Silas were imprisoned, bound in chains after being falsely accused and beaten for preaching the gospel. They had every reason to feel defeated, discouraged, and hopeless. Yet instead of sinking into despair, they made a radical choice—they began to praise and worship God. In the darkest hour, locked away in the depths of a prison, they lifted their voices in songs of faith. This act of worship did more than strengthen their spirits—it triggered a miraculous breakthrough. The prison shook, their chains fell off, and the doors flung open. Their praise set them free.

This story in Acts 16 is more than a historical account—it is a blueprint for victory in relationships that feel trapped or weighed down. We have seen how praise and worship break the chains that can bind a marriage. Many couples experience emotional, spiritual, and relational struggles that feel like imprisonment—silent resentment, unresolved conflict, financial pressures, or deep wounds from past mistakes. These invisible chains keep love from flourishing, trapping couples in cycles of disappointment and frustration. But like Paul and Silas, couples have the power to shift their atmosphere through worship.

When Kathleen and I face moments of strain, when pressure seems to tighten around us, we have learned to follow Paul and Silas' example. Instead of arguing or retreating into silence, we lift our voices in praise. Worship reminds us that God is greater than our struggles, that His presence is enough to bring renewal, and that chains—whether emotional, spiritual, or relational—are no match for His power. Just as the prison doors swung open, worship opens the door to healing, reconciliation, and peace.

Praise disrupts the enemy's plans. The devil thrives on division, resentment, and hopelessness, but worship declares that love, faith, and grace will prevail. When couples choose praise over bitterness, they invite God's presence into their relationship, creating an environment where healing can begin. Kathleen and I have experienced this time and again—worship softens our hearts, breaks down barriers, and allows us to reconnect in ways that words alone cannot.

Another profound lesson from Paul and Silas is their unwavering faith. They praised before their breakthrough, not after. Couples often wait for circumstances to improve before turning to worship, but true faith praises God in advance. Worship shifts focus away from the problem and toward God's promises. We have discovered that when we worship even when situations seem uncertain, we find peace long before a resolution arrives.

Praise also reinforces unity. Paul and Silas were not alone in their worship—they sang together. Worship has the power to knit hearts together, creating a deeper level of emotional and spiritual connection. When couples praise as one, they fight battles together instead of against each other. We have learned that worship is not just an individual act—it is a shared experience that strengthens the foundation of love.

For couples struggling, feeling bound by difficulties or weighed down by circumstances, the answer is clear. Praise breaks chains. Worship is not just a remedy—it is a weapon. Paul and Silas didn't just survive their prison—they walked out free, victorious, and stronger than before. Couples who embrace worship in their relationship will find the same freedom. Love will no longer feel trapped—it will thrive, empowered by the presence of God.

David's relationship with God was deeply intertwined with worship. He praised God in moments of triumph and moments of despair, dancing without shame before the Lord, writing psalms of thanksgiving, and trusting God through every season of his life. His example teaches that worship must be consistent, not just reserved for times of hardship. Kathleen and I have made worship a lifestyle, ensuring that it is a daily practice, not just something we turn to in times of need. We sing together in the car, pray before meals, declare God's goodness in casual conversations, and allow worship to be a natural part of our relationship.

David understood something profound—the power of music as a tool for healing, transformation, and spiritual warfare. In 1 Samuel 16, Saul was tormented by an evil spirit, restless and unable to find peace. His servants recognized that music could soothe him, and they sought out a skilled musician to play for the king. That musician was David, a young shepherd who had already developed a deep relationship with God through worship. When David played his harp, something remarkable happened—the torment lifted, and Saul found relief.

David's music wasn't just entertainment; it carried the presence of God. It wasn't the sound alone that healed Saul—it was the anointing behind it. Worship has that same power today. Kathleen and I have discovered that praise and worship are more than just expressions of faith—they are healing forces in a relationship. Just as David's music drove out the darkness surrounding Saul, worship can drive out tension, fear, and division in a marriage.

There have been moments when we faced difficulties, when emotions were heavy and words felt inadequate. Instead of allowing frustration to take root, we turned to worship. Playing music, singing together, or simply filling our home with praise changed the atmosphere. It was as if the heaviness lifted, much like Saul's torment dissipated when David played his harp. Worship does not just soothe the mind; it shifts the spiritual environment.

Music carries power beyond human understanding. Worship realigns hearts, replaces anxiety with peace, and invites God's presence to work in ways words alone cannot. Saul could not reason his way out of torment, but the presence of God in David's music ushered in relief. Couples facing struggles in their relationship often try to resolve things through endless conversations, but sometimes, the breakthrough comes not through words but through worship.

We have made praise and worship a lifestyle, knowing that it is not just a way to celebrate good times but a way to overcome challenges. Whether playing music softly in the background, singing together while driving, or allowing worship to lead us into prayer, we have seen how it strengthens our bond and deepens our connection to God. Worship does not erase struggles, but it changes the way couples face them.

David's harp did more than calm Saul—it carried God's presence. Praise and worship can do the same in a relationship. They bring restoration, peace, and unity where division once threatened to take hold. The enemy cannot thrive in an environment filled with God's presence, and worship ensures that the battles within a relationship are not fought alone but with God leading the way.

Beyond biblical examples, there are countless practical ways couples experience the power of worship in their relationship. Many couples struggle with communication breakdowns, misunderstandings, and unspoken frustrations. Worship creates an environment where healing can take place. Instead of allowing resentment to build, praise opens the door for humility and reconciliation. Kathleen and I have faced moments when emotions were high and words alone could not resolve the issue, but singing together brought understanding where conversations failed.

Worship acts as a reset button, shifting focus from problems to promises. Instead of dwelling on anxieties, worship reminds couples that God is their provider, their healer, and their guide. We have turned to worship when uncertainty about the future weighed heavily on us, and every time, we were reminded that God has already made a way.

Worship also strengthens emotional and spiritual intimacy. When couples praise together, they connect on a deeper level, inviting God into their bond. Worship removes pride, softens hearts, and realigns priorities. We have felt the difference worship makes in our relationship—it helps us remain patient, attentive, and in sync with each other.

Praise and worship are not just optional elements of faith—they are mandatory for couples who want to thrive. Worship is the weapon that defeats division, the shield that protects relationships, and the glue that holds love together. Kathleen and I have committed to making worship the foundation of our marriage, knowing that through it, we remain spiritually anchored, emotionally connected, and unwavering in faith.

Sunday afternoons were sacred in our home. After church, after the warmth of a home-cooked meal and the sweetness of dessert, we would gather around the piano, letting melodies weave their way into our hearts. Music was not just a pastime—it was worship, it was connection, it was the way we anchored ourselves in God's presence.

Kathleen loved those moments. From our earlier years of marriage, she delighted in hearing me sing with the children, finding joy in the way music carried our faith and wrapped it in harmonies. Our first daughter, Karleen, and I spent endless hours at the piano, pouring our hearts into song. The other children joined in as well, though Karleen and I shared a special musical bond, one that deepened when we wrote a song together—*Take Me In To Your Presence, I Want to See Your Glory*.

It was more than just lyrics and chords. It was a prayer, a longing, an invitation.

That afternoon, as we sang, something indescribable happened.

The presence of God filled the room, thick and undeniable. It wasn't just a feeling—it was a reality, as tangible as the hands we lifted in surrender. It was the same presence that had come down in crusades, in church services, in the moments before marriage when ministry took me across the world. But now, here in our home, in the intimate setting of our family worship, it consumed us.

Tears fell freely as we worshiped, as we allowed the weight of His glory to settle upon us. It wasn't rehearsed. It wasn't planned. It was simply a moment where heaven met earth, where our song became more than words—it became an offering.

But it did not stop there.

I had a meeting in Finland, a gathering unlike any other. As we sang this song—a melody born of reverence and surrender—something extraordinary happened. The atmosphere shifted, thick with a holiness so tangible it felt as if it could be grasped, held in our hands. It was a presence so powerful that every breath carried the weight of divine encounter, every note of the song became an invitation for heaven to touch earth.

And then, the floodgates opened.

Over 150 people rushed to the altar, drawn not by mere emotion but by the undeniable pull of the Spirit. They came with open hearts, with eyes lifted toward heaven, responding to something greater than themselves. And in those sacred moments, about 25 began manifesting as though they were demon possessed, as the presence of God descended upon us with an intensity that sent ripples through the room. The air was thick—so thick you could cut it with a knife. A holy silence, a reverent trembling, a cry of surrender—it was a sacred outpouring, an encounter so profound that it was beyond words.

Kathleen and I have always known that worship is not simply about songs—it is about surrender, about opening the door for heaven to meet us where we stand. That night in Finland was yet another confirmation that when hearts are open and voices are raised in true devotion, the presence of God does not merely visit—it inhabits, it transforms, it awakens.

I was speaking in Holland at a church, filled with over a fifteen hundred souls gathered under the great arches of faith. I stood before them, heart open, voice lifted, and as I sang the song *"Take Me In To Your Presence, I Want to See Your Glory,"* our family wrote, something greater than myself moved in the room. It was not just music—it was an invitation, a whisper from heaven calling them forward.

One by one, hands thrown into the heavens, eyes welling with tears, over two hundred and fifty people stepped forward, drawn not by spectacle, but by something unseen yet deeply felt. A sacred hush fell over the congregation as the presence of God descended, wrapping around them like a warm embrace, like a whisper that assured, *"I am here."*

I saw hearts break open, burdens lifted. In that moment, it did not matter where they had been, what they had done—only that they were here, standing in His presence, utterly surrendered.

I was at a church in Ottawa, it happened again. As we sang that same song *"Take Me In To Your Presence, I Want to See Your Glory,"* the first five rows—an entire wave of people—fell under the power of God. It was not chaos, nor confusion, but a divine encounter. It was as though an unseen hand had moved through the air, catching them in an embrace so mighty, so full of mercy, that their knees buckled under the weight of it.

Some wept openly, faces buried in trembling hands. Others knelt, as if suddenly aware that they were standing on holy ground. And still others simply stood, eyes closed, their hearts lifted like vessels receiving an overflow.

I did not know what each person had carried into that room. I did not know the depths of their pain, the prayers whispered in private, the doubts wrestled with in the quiet corners of their minds. But in that moment, I knew one thing: they were seen. They were known. And they were loved beyond measure.

AS FOR ME AND MY SPOUSE WE WILL PRAISE THE LORD

In every city, in every church, I sang that song *"Take Me In To Your Presence, I Want to See Your Glory"*. And every time, God moved. It was never about the notes or the melody—it was about the call. And when He called, they came.

The church in Swift Current was expectant. There was an atmosphere of hunger, a yearning for something beyond words, beyond routine. As I stood before them and lifted my voice in worship, something mighty swept through the room.

It was not just emotion—it was God's presence. It was power.

I saw it before I fully understood it. The worship team, their voices raised in adoration, suddenly stilled. They fell back under the weight of His glory. Even the pastor's wife, a pillar in the congregation, found herself overcome, caught in a moment where human strength was no match for the divine. It wasn't chaos—it was surrender. It was holy.

By the time the night service began, the church could barely contain the crowd. People pressed in, shoulder to shoulder, filling every available space, their hearts eager, expectant. And as the call to worship rose again, heaven responded.

People dropped under the presence of God, not in fear, not in confusion, but in awe. Some sank to their knees, hands raised, tears streaming down their faces. Others lay still, caught in a holy hush, as if resting in the arms of the One who had called them there.

It was a night where walls could not confine the move of God. Where hunger met fulfillment. Where worship was not just sung—it was lived.

But it did not stop there.

Germany was cold that season, the kind of chill that pressed against the skin and settled deep into the bones. But inside the church, there was warmth—something greater than heat, something sacred.

Among the many who had gathered, there was a woman with eyes full of longing. She had traveled over seven hours to be there, carrying both anticipation and a quiet resolve. A year earlier, she had surrendered her heart to Jesus at the same church I spoke at, and now, in the depths of winter, she wanted to seal her faith—choosing to be baptized in the icy waters of the Baltic Sea.

But she had not come alone. Beside her stood her boyfriend, a bodybuilder—a man accustomed to strength, control, resistance. He had heard the stories, whispers of God's power moving through the meetings, and he came forward, determined to stand. To resist. To prove that no unseen force could move him.

He squared his shoulders, planted his feet, and waited as I picked him out from the crowd and asked him to join me at the altar.

As I lifted my voice, worshiping Jesus, something unseen filled the space. It was thick, tangible, pressing in like a holy atmosphere. And then, as I glanced across the room—he was no longer standing.

There, on the floor, lay the man who had come prepared to resist. He had expected a push, a hand, a force that could be explained. But no one had touched him. No words had been spoken over him. He had simply fallen—yielding to something far greater than himself.

Silence swept over the room, yet it was a silence alive with awe. Around him, people knelt, worship continued, and in that sacred stillness, something deeper than human strength was at work. It was not humiliation—it was revelation. The presence of God had moved, had called, had embraced, and he had fallen not because he was weak, but because he had encountered a strength beyond muscles, beyond resistance, beyond anything he had ever known.

For a man who had spent his life mastering control, this moment was not loss—it was discovery. He asked to received Jesus into his heart and became radical in wanting the world to know Jesus is alive.

AS FOR ME AND MY SPOUSE WE WILL PRAISE THE LORD

As worship continued, I knew—this was why she had brought him. Not just to witness, not just to accompany, but to encounter. And that night, he did.

In India at a crusade unfolding with power, with worship rising like incense into the night sky. As we sang, and I started to preach the Word of God, with voices mingled, hands lifted, in the midst of it all, a group of people started dancing wildly, disrupting the meeting. At first, it seemed like distraction, a force working against what God was doing. But soon, I would learn the truth.

Someone rushed up to me, breathless with wonder. Their words were staggering—"*four adults, paralyzed from birth, had been healed while you was speaking.*"

I felt my spirit pause. Not in hesitation, but in reverence. The presence of God had moved beyond what was seen, beyond what was expected. Healing had touched lives while the words were still on my lips. We had many salvations and healings that followed that meeting.

Then, an invitation came. The village of those healed wanted to celebrate. And so, I went.

Nothing could have prepared me for the welcome that awaited me. As I arrived, over five hundred people filled the streets, their voices lifted in song, their feet moving in dance. The sound of drums echoed through the air, a rhythm of joy that pulsed through every soul present.

They surrounded me, their faces full of gratitude, their hands reaching out with garlands, placing them around my neck in a gesture of honour and respect. But in that moment, I knew what had to be said.

"It was not me. It was Jesus."

I lifted my hands, gently removing the weight of their praise from myself and placing it where it belonged. I reminded them, it is Christ who heals, who moves, who touches hearts and bodies with power beyond human strength.

And there, among the singing, the dancing, the celebration, the truth was spoken—not in whispers, but in joyful proclamation. Not in quiet reflection, but in the exuberance of a people who had seen, had witnessed, had received.

This was not just healing—it was a testimony. It was a village transformed, a moment that could not be explained, only embraced. And as we worshiped, as we praised, as we declared the name of Jesus, His presence did not wane. It increased.

The crusade in St. Kitts was unlike anything I had witnessed before. The air was thick with expectation, hearts turned toward heaven in worship. As voices rose, as hands lifted, the presence of God descended—powerful, undeniable.

Hundreds surged forward, drawn not by emotion alone, but by something greater—a divine pull that called them into surrender. And as the presence intensified, the unseen world responded.

Demonic manifestations erupted among the crowd, voices shrieking, bodies convulsing as darkness resisted the light that had come. Without hesitation, several were led behind the platform where the power of God set them free—chains broken, oppression lifted. It was a battleground, but one where victory had already been declared.

Yet beyond the crusades, beyond the miracles and deliverance, there was a deeper presence—one that guided our own lives, our family.

As Kathleen and I lifted our voices in praise, we felt it—the spiritual resilience rising within us, the sacred clarity that came when we worshiped together. It was in those moments of surrender that God spoke, giving direction not just for the ministry, but for our home.

Seven children—a blessing, a calling. And yet, how does one raise them? How does one shape hearts to know Him, to follow Him? The blueprint did not come from books, from opinions, from earthly wisdom—it came from the presence of God.

It was there, in the stillness of worship, that the Holy Spirit led us, guided us, counselled and instructed us. It was in His presence that unity was forged in our marriage—not just as husband and wife, but as partners in faith.

The world may say love is tested through trials, through hardship, through perseverance. And it is. But we have found that love—true, lasting, unshakable love—is strengthened in worship.

A couple who praises together stays together.

It is worship that keeps us bound not only to each other but to Him. It is worship that transforms ordinary days into holy moments. And it is worship that continues to lead us forward, step by step, surrender by surrender.

PRAISE UNVEILED

There are moments in life when it feels as though heaven has gone silent, when prayers seem to echo unanswered, when desperation knocks at the door but there is no visible relief. We have lived through those moments—times when food was scarce, when provision seemed distant, when faith was tested in the most practical ways. It was in those seasons that we learned the greatest lesson of all: praise is not meant for the easy times; it is built for the storms.

Coming back from the mission field should have felt like a homecoming, a return to stability, but instead, it brought uncertainty. We found ourselves struggling, barely able to afford food, relying on the kindness of friends who would bring leftovers from a Chinese restaurant—buckets filled like scraps meant for stray animals. But never once did we complain. We knew something others might not understand—praise is not dependent on circumstances; it is a declaration of trust, a refusal to let hardship dictate our faith.

There was one particular Sunday that stands as a testament to how praise operates even when logic says otherwise. Kathleen and I had nothing left but a single twenty-dollar bill. It wasn't just money—it was a lifeline, the last tangible security we had. That morning, standing together in the kitchen, I felt something stir in my spirit. I heard the Lord whisper, *Give it.* It wasn't a command; it was an invitation, an opportunity to step into complete trust. But how do you give when you have nothing? How do you release what little you hold when need is staring back at you?

I turned to Kathleen, asking what she thought. Her answer was simple, unwavering. *"Do as the Lord tells you to do."* No persuasion, no debate, just faith. It wasn't the answer I wanted, but it was the truth I needed.

At church, as the offering bucket passed by, the internal battle continued. *What if we needed this tomorrow? What if this was the one thing between us and hunger? What if this is a mistake?* But the same voice whispered, *Give it.* Again, I turned to Kathleen, hoping for a different response, but she simply repeated, *"Do as the Lord tells you to do."* No escape, no excuse—I had my answer. So, I let it go. As the offering bucket passed by, I thought maybe the Lord was saying "take $20.00" instead of give $20.00.

After the service, the pastor asked to see me before the evening service. My heart sank. *This must mean trouble.* But when I stood before him, what he said shocked me. He said, *"I have never done this in all my ministry life, but I want to give you a personal check for five hundred dollars."* In 1997, five hundred dollars wasn't just five hundred dollars —it was provision beyond what we could have imagined. That twenty-dollar bill wasn't a loss; it was a seed, a declaration of trust that was met with divine provision.

This moment solidified something that we had been learning all along: when God speaks, we praise Him. Not because the answer is immediate, not because the struggle disappears, but because He is always moving, always working, even when we cannot see it. Praise reminds us that the obstacles are never the focus—the faithfulness of God is.

AS FOR ME AND MY SPOUSE WE WILL PRAISE THE LORD

We don't praise because life is perfect; we praise because God is. When the cupboards are empty, when the bills pile up, when uncertainty stares us down, praise is what shifts our perspective. It keeps our eyes on the Provider rather than the problem. It breaks the stronghold of fear, silences doubt, and invites heaven to move.

We have seen this principle work over and over again. Whether it was unexpected provision, strength in hardship, or doors opening when we least expected them, praise has always preceded breakthrough. Even when life seemed unfair, even when suffering felt unbearable, praise kept our hearts aligned with heaven.

If we had only praised when things were easy, we would have missed the miracle. But because we praised in the storm, we saw the hand of God move in ways that still leave us in awe. That Sunday wasn't just a moment—it was a lesson, one that continues to shape our faith today. We don't wait for answers to praise; we praise because the answer is already written in His goodness.

God requires praise because it is the purest expressions of love, trust, and surrender. Praise is not just about music or rituals—it is an act of recognizing His greatness, aligning ourselves with His will, and declaring His authority over all things. From the beginning of creation to the eternal praise seen in heaven, praise has always been central to the relationship between God and His people.

Throughout Scripture, we see that praise is not just encouraged—it is commanded. When Moses led Israel out of Egypt, God reminded them that their freedom was not just about escaping oppression but about living a life of devotion to Him. Praise was woven into the fabric of their identity, a reminder that they belonged to God. The Psalms continually call for praise, commanding all creation to glorify the Lord. Praise is not just for moments of joy—it is for every season, whether in times of celebration or trial.

PRAISE UNVEILED

In Revelation, the heavenly realm is described as a place where worship never ceases. The twenty-four elders lay their crowns before God, the four living creatures cry out day and night, "Holy, holy, holy is the Lord God Almighty." This unceasing praise reflects the truth that worship is not just an earthly practice—it is the eternal response to God's holiness. If praise fills heaven, then it must be essential here on earth.

Praise is also a form of spiritual warfare. When Jehoshaphat faced an overwhelming enemy, he did not send his soldiers first—he sent worshipers ahead of the army. As they praised God, their enemies turned on each other, and victory was won without Judah lifting a sword. Worship shifts battles from physical to spiritual, allowing God to fight on our behalf.

Praise create intimacy with God. Just as a relationship cannot thrive without communication, faith cannot deepen without worship. Praise is our way of drawing near to Him, acknowledging His love, power, and presence in our lives. Kathleen and I have seen how worship transforms our home—when we praise together, we feel God's peace filling every corner, reminding us that He is at the center of our marriage.

Praise is not just a practice—it is the foundation of faith. It is how we declare who God is, how we stay connected to Him, and how we align ourselves with His purposes. He does not require worship because He needs validation—He commands it because it is the key to experiencing His presence, walking in victory, and living in the fullness of His promises. Worship is not just something we do—it is who we are called to be.

Praise is a powerful way we connect with God, yet they serve distinct purposes. They are not mere traditions or religious rituals; they are invitations to experience God's presence in a profound way. Kathleen and I have come to understand that praise and worship are not things we do to appease God—they are gifts He has given us to deepen our relationship with Him.

Praise is the act of exalting God for His goodness, power, and faithfulness. It is often expressive, filled with joy and gratitude, declaring who God is and what He has done. Praise acknowledges His past victories, His unfailing love, and His promises fulfilled. In Scripture, we see praise being offered in song, dance, loud proclamations, and even instrumental music. When David danced before the Lord, it was an uninhibited display of praise—he wasn't concerned about appearances, only about honouring God. Praise is like cheering at a sports event when your team has won, except it is directed at the One who never loses. It is a way to celebrate His victories, His goodness, and His faithfulness.

Worship, on the other hand, goes deeper. While praise often focuses on thanking God for His actions, worship is about surrendering to who He is. It is an intimate act of devotion, a declaration that God is Lord over our lives. Worship is reverence, a recognition of His holiness, and an offering of ourselves to Him. When Abraham was willing to sacrifice Isaac, it was an act of worship—he trusted that God's plan was greater than his own understanding. Worship is not always loud and energetic; sometimes it is quiet, reflective, and deeply personal. It is about aligning our hearts with His, submitting our desires to His will, and acknowledging that He is worthy, regardless of our circumstances.

God asks us to praise Him, but He does not demand it out of obligation or need. He is not like earthly rulers who seek validation or recognition—He commands praise because it draws us closer to Him. Praise is transformative; it is impossible to be in His presence and remain unchanged. When we praise, our hearts shift, our minds clear, and our spirits realign with His truth. Praise lifts us out of discouragement, reminding us of His faithfulness, while worship deepens our trust in Him, keeping us anchored in His love.

Kathleen and I have learned that praise and worship is more than just a church practice—it is a lifestyle. We praise when we wake up, we worship in quiet moments, and we integrate these acts into our marriage. Praise is not about obligation; it is about the relationship. God does not require worship because He is lacking—it is because He knows we need it to remain connected to Him

Praise is more than expressions of faith; they are the foundation for healing, restoration, and peace in a relationship. Kathleen and I have discovered that praise is not just a choice—it is essential. It has become the safeguard that protects our love, the force that dissolves tension, and the practice that keeps us connected to God in every season. Worship is not optional for a thriving relationship—it is necessary.

One of the most powerful aspects of praise is its ability to shift focus. Conflict and frustration can cloud a relationship, causing couples to dwell on problems instead of solutions. Praise redirects attention from challenges to gratitude, turning moments of anger into moments of surrender. We have experienced times when emotions ran high, but worship became our refuge. Instead of engaging in negativity, we lifted our voices in praise, allowing God's presence to dissolve frustration and bring clarity.

We praise Him in good times, and we praise Him in bad times. We lift His name even when everything in us feels weary, even when life presses down with unanswered prayers, prolonged waiting, and doors that seem forever shut. Praise is not just for the victories—it is for the valleys. It is in those moments of disappointment, when breakthroughs seem distant, when the longing for healing, provision, or direction feels unanswered, that we must press in the most.

Kathleen and I have learned that praise gets God's attention. It is not just an act—it is a declaration of trust, an offering of faith when circumstances try to shake it. We have praised Him in our joys, in the sacred milestones of our lives—when we got married, when we held our firstborn in our arms. But we have also praised Him in the struggles, when we barely had enough money to put gasoline in our car just to visit our parents who lived only an hour and a half away. We have praised Him when the car broke down, when life felt uncertain, when the road ahead seemed impossible.

One night, we experienced this firsthand. We were leaving my parents' house with our four children, the drive stretching a little over an hour. Halfway home, on a long, dark road, the van ran out of gasoline. The gas gauge was broken—we hadn't known. At first, we kept trying to start the engine, praying for a miracle, hoping that somehow, it would restart. But nothing happened. The battery eventually died, the engine refusing to turn.

I stepped out, leaving the lights on so that no one would hit our van in the darkness. I had no choice but to flag down a stranger. In that moment, I had to believe that this man would not harm me, that he would not abandon me somewhere far away, leaving Kathleen and our children alone in the dark. I had to trust that God had sent help.

He took me to a gas station and brought me back to the van. Before leaving, he asked, "Is everything good now?" and then drove off. I filled the gas tank, went inside, and turned the key—but now, the battery was completely dead. The keys wouldn't even turn.

Kathleen and I sat there, staring at the situation before us, knowing that human logic had run out of solutions. And so, we did the only thing we knew to do—we prayed, we praised. For ten minutes, in the middle of the night, on a silent road with our children fast asleep, we lifted our voices in faith. We spoke His name, we declared His power, we worshipped with everything in us.

And then, in the name of Jesus, I turned the key one more time. The van started.

We drove all the way home without another issue.

That night was not just about a van—it was a reminder. A lesson that praise isn't just for the moments when life makes sense. Praise is for the moments when nothing does. Praise is for the times when logic tells us it is hopeless, when circumstances tell us to give up. Because praise isn't about what we see—it is about declaring who He is. It is a weapon, a force, a connection to the God who always shows up.

And He does. Every time!

So we praise Him in the storms, and we praise Him in the sunshine. Because no matter where we stand, no matter how dark the road may seem—He is worthy.

Praise invites the presence of God into every situation. Scripture tells us that God inhabits the praises of His people. This truth has reshaped how we approach difficult moments. Instead of relying on our own ability to resolve tension, we bring praise into our relationship, trusting that God will guide us. The peace that follows is undeniable—praise does not just ease emotions; it transforms hearts.

A critical reason praise brings healing is that it fosters humility. Pride often stands in the way of resolution, making it difficult to apologize, listen, or forgive. Praise naturally requires surrender. Kathleen and I have found that when we sing or pray together, barriers fall, and humility takes the lead. Praise softens us, allowing grace to replace defensiveness and love to override frustration.

Praise also releases emotional burdens. The weight of stress, uncertainty, and fear can create distance between couples. Praise is the place where those burdens are lifted. We have used praise to shift our perspective, turning overwhelming moments into moments of peace. Praise reminds us that God is in control, reassuring us that no challenge is too great for Him.

One morning after returning from India, my heart was full. I had witnessed miracles, seen lives transformed, and experienced the power of God in ways that left me in awe. It had been an incredible time of ministry, and as I landed back home, exhausted yet overflowing with gratitude, I felt deeply assured that God was moving.

At the time, Kathleen and I owned a small retail store. During my trip, I had purchased a box of beautifully carved marble elephants—intricate designs with tiny baby elephants sculpted within the larger ones. Each piece was heavy, elegant, and held significant value. I had planned to sell them in our store, estimating their worth at around $25 back then—today, they might be worth nearly double.

After a long flight and an exhausting drive home from the airport, I was too tired to unload them. I decided to leave the box of elephants in our van, thinking I'd move them the following morning. But when morning came, the van was gone—stolen overnight, along with every single elephant inside.

I was shocked. Frustrated. Confused. How could this happen right after returning from doing the Lord's work? I wrestled with the anger rising within me, trying to understand why such a loss would come after a season of faithful ministry. But Kathleen and I refused to dwell in disappointment. Instead, we turned to praise.

We lifted our voices and declared God's sovereignty, knowing deep down that He always has something greater in store.

The police were involved, the insurance processed, and soon we received a check—an amount over three times more than the actual value of the van. Shortly after, the van was located at the scene of a robbery in town, completely written off. But by then, we had been blessed with more than enough to purchase a better vehicle.

Within six months later, the new van was stolen. And again, we were blessed with a check that exceeded what we originally paid for it. We praised God even more for His faithfulness.

Through every trial, God had a plan—one far greater than what we could have imagined.

Eventually, we purchased a brand-new van, fresh from the lot with only five kilometers on it. We drove that vehicle for six years, trusting in the Lord's provision through every season. And then, one day, Kathleen and I both heard the same prompting in our spirits—the Lord was asking us to give it away. Without hesitation, we donated the van to a church, knowing that He would always provide.

We have seen firsthand that sowing seeds, living with a heart of gratitude, and choosing to praise the Lord brings immeasurable blessings.

Praise is not a response to good circumstances—it is a declaration of trust in every season, whether in gain or loss, in certainty or uncertainty. It is our testimony that God is always working, always faithful, always leading us toward something greater than we could have planned ourselves.

Spiritual intimacy is deepened through praise and trust is developed that God is in control. Singing, praying, and praising together create a bond that is stronger than words. We have seen how worship allows us to connect in ways that surpass ordinary communication. Praise in a relationship builds a unity that withstands trials and reinforces trust in God's plan.

Praise is also proclaiming victory over struggles. It is not just a response to blessings—it is a declaration of faith. Kathleen and I use praise as a way to speak life over our relationship, believing that no matter what comes, God is faithful. Praise shifts discouragement into encouragement, defeat into hope, and uncertainty into confidence in His promises.

Praise in a relationship is not just beneficial—it is essential. It creates an atmosphere of healing, restores peace, and keeps love anchored in God's presence. We continue to build our lives around praise, knowing that it is not just a practice but the foundation that ensures lasting connection, unity, and unwavering faith.

THE HEARTBEAT OF HEAVEN

Worship is the heartbeat of heaven that has been the cornerstone of our lives, the sacred thread woven through every joy and trial, binding us to God and to each other. It is more than an act—it is a posture, a way of living, a continual surrender that transforms ordinary moments into divine encounters.

In worship, we have found strength when weary, direction when uncertain, and peace when storms have threatened to shake us. It is in those moments—those quiet whispers of devotion—that God speaks, reminding us that His presence is not only with us, but guiding us, shaping us, and leading us deeper into His will.

Each morning, as we lift our voices in praise, we step into His promises, into the blessing declared in Numbers 6:24-26—the assurance of His protection, His grace, His ever-present peace. Worship is not just something we do; it is the place where we dwell. It is our refuge, our sanctuary, our reminder that no matter what life holds, God is near, sustaining us, equipping us for what is ahead.

At its core, worship is about devotion—wholehearted, sincere, and unwavering. It is rooted in love, allegiance, and the unshakable truth that our lives are meant to reflect His glory. It is our response to His goodness, our declaration of His holiness. And it is in worship that we are reminded that faith is not passive—it is active, lived out in every word spoken, every decision made, every step taken.

Worship has strengthened our marriage, creating a bond that is not merely sustained by affection, but anchored in faith. It has shaped how we love, how we listen, how we lead. And as we continue to seek Him together, we walk forward in confidence, knowing that a life of worship is a life of blessing—one where His presence is ever near, His voice ever clear, His love ever faithful.

True worship permeates every aspect of life, shaping the way we think, speak, and act. It is not confined to Sunday services or moments of prayer; it is a continual offering—a lifestyle of surrender and devotion.

Romans 12:1-2 calls us to present our bodies as living sacrifices, an invitation to let worship be reflected in the way we live. It is not just about lifting our hands in praise, but about surrendering our hearts, our choices, our daily interactions to God's will. This kind of worship is holistic, extending beyond words into action, into love, into service. Hebrews 13:15-16 reinforces this truth, encouraging us to worship not only with our lips but with our lives—offering praise and doing good, ensuring that worship is an active expression of faith, not just an outward gesture.

One of the foundational principles of worship is that it must remain God-centered and God-directed. Psalms 115:1 echoes this beautifully, reminding us that worship is not about exalting ourselves but about glorifying God alone. His love and faithfulness are the reason we praise, the anchor that keeps our hearts in alignment with His will.

Worship is not dependent on circumstances or fleeting emotions; it is rooted in truth, in an unwavering recognition of God's sovereignty. Revelation 4-5 paints a powerful image of heavenly worship—creation bowing in reverence, declaring His majesty in complete adoration. It is a reminder that worship is not just a choice but a response to His greatness, a reflection of what is already happening in heaven.

As Kathleen and I embrace worship as a way of life, we have witnessed how it transforms everything. It strengthens our faith, deepens our marriage, and aligns our steps with divine purpose. Worship is where we receive wisdom, where we find peace, where we are reminded that we are not alone in this journey. It is the place where miracles happen, where direction is given, where God's presence becomes undeniable.

This is why we worship—not just in moments of need or celebration, but in every breath, every step, every decision. Because when worship becomes a way of life, everything else falls into place.

Christ remains at the center of all worship, the One who makes our praise acceptable before God. Without Him, worship is incomplete, lacking the depth and connection that His sacrifice secured for us. Hebrews 9:22 reminds us that redemption required His blood, that it is through Him our worship is made pure, holy, and pleasing to the Father. Worship is not simply an act—it is a communion with the One who has bridged the gap between heaven and earth, inviting us into His presence with confidence. Hebrews 4:14-16 reassures us that Christ, our High Priest, grants us direct access to the Father, drawing us into the heart of true worship.

Yet worship is not always easy. There are moments when weariness takes hold, when disappointment dulls the desire to lift our voices. Life's trials can sometimes make it feel easier to remain silent rather than to worship. But Isaiah 42:6-7 reminds us that Christ is our covenant, our binding connection to God, sustaining us through every valley and every victory. Worship is not merely about singing songs—it is about surrender, about shaping our lives to reflect His love, His truth, and His righteousness in all that we do.

THE HEARTBEAT OF HEAVEN

Carrying worship throughout the day requires intentionality. It is easy to compartmentalize worship into designated times—Sunday mornings, moments of prayer—but true worship is continuous, woven into the fabric of our daily lives. One of the simplest ways to stay immersed in His presence is through music, allowing it to settle into the heart and spirit, becoming a quiet echo of praise throughout the day.

I often condition my mind by playing the same song repeatedly, letting its melody and words soak into my spirit. It is not just sound—it becomes presence, a lingering whisper of heaven that carries me through the day. In the middle of work, in moments of stillness, even amidst the noise of life, I hear it. The melody rises softly, reminding me that I am never far from worship, never far from His presence.

Worship transforms everything—it shifts atmospheres, renews hearts, and strengthens faith. It is not just what we do; it is who we are called to be. And when worship becomes the rhythm of our lives, we find ourselves walking in divine alignment, constantly aware of His nearness, constantly reminded that we are held by grace.

Even as I work, as my hands move and my thoughts focus on tasks, the song remains. It rises softly within me, as if heaven itself is singing it back to me. I hear it, not with my ears, but with my heart. It becomes a thread that ties me to worship, an anchor that holds me steady in His presence.

This practice is more than repetition—it is devotion. It is a way of staying connected, of keeping my spirit lifted, of ensuring that no matter where I am or what I am doing, worship is never far from me.

Because when my heart is tuned to His song, my soul can rest. My spirit can rejoice. And I can walk through each moment knowing that I am surrounded by the presence of God.

Psalms 47:1-2 encourages us to clap our hands and shout unto God with triumph, demonstrating that worship is not confined to passive reflection but includes active engagement. We weave worship into everything we do—whether through spoken praise, quiet prayers, or acts of kindness. We have found that keeping worship at the forefront of our lives allows us to experience God's presence in a way that transforms our hearts and minds.

Worship is a dialogue, a response to God's holiness, and an acknowledgment of His mercy and grace. It is a sacred space where love and allegiance meet divine truth, shaping the way we live, love, and serve. We hold onto worship as our source of strength, knowing that it sustains us through every challenge and lifts us into a deeper experience of God's presence. Worship is more than an act—it is the heartbeat of faith, the foundation of unity, and the source of unshakable strength.

Worship has always been at the center of Kathleen and my spiritual journey. It is more than an act of devotion—it is the foundation upon which we build our faith, find our strength, and sustain our connection to God. Worship feeds our spirits, allowing us to live in alignment with His will. The principles that govern worship ensure that it remains pure, transformative, and deeply rooted in biblical truth.

There have been moments—ordinary, everyday moments—when the Holy Spirit gently nudges me into worship. Whether I'm driving in my car, working out at the gym, or walking through a store, I feel that quiet yet undeniable pull, a whisper that calls me to lift my heart in praise. And when I do, something shifts.

The presence of God manifests, turning even the most mundane spaces into sacred encounters. Worship is not just a song or a moment in church—it is a lifestyle, a constant invitation to dwell in His presence, no matter where I am.

And in that surrender, favour follows. We have experienced unexpected blessings—being bumped up to first class flights, finding the clothes we need on sale, receiving discounted rates on trips, and being met with surprises we never anticipated. But beyond the gifts, beyond the provisions, there is something far greater: the undeniable reminder that when we worship, we align ourselves with His abundance, His goodness, His divine orchestration over our lives.

Because in worship, we don't just express gratitude—we step into the overflow of His grace.

Worship is the very essence of our faith, shaping not only our hearts but the way we walk, live, and serve. It is a transformative experience, refining us daily, drawing us deeper into communion with God. Hebrews 13:20-21 reassures us that God perfects us in every good work, preparing us to fulfill His divine will. Worship is not merely a moment—it is an ongoing surrender that allows us to be molded by His presence.

At the heart of worship is a fundamental truth: it must always be God-centered and God-directed. Worship is never about seeking personal reward or chasing fleeting emotions. It is about standing in awe of His majesty, offering Him the highest honor. Revelation 4-5 paints a breathtaking picture of heavenly worship, where creation itself resounds with praise. That vision reminds us that true worship is about exalting Him above all else, ensuring that our focus remains unwavering, undistracted by the noise of the world.

Equally vital is the principle that worship must remain Christ-focused. Without Him, worship lacks the bridge that allows us to step into the presence of the Father. Hebrews 9:22 speaks to this necessity—His sacrifice is what purifies and makes our worship acceptable. First Timothy 2:5 underscores this truth, declaring that Christ is our only mediator, the One through whom we have access to the Father. Worship is more than an expression of devotion—it is a declaration of gratitude for the redeeming power of Christ, recognizing that without Him, we would stand distant from God's holiness.

Every time we worship, we step into alignment with heaven. We are reminded of His faithfulness, His sovereignty, His unchanging love.

Worship is a foundation, a way of life, a continual offering that allows us to walk in divine purpose, experiencing the fullness of His presence in ways that transform our very being.

Worship must also be Spirit-led and Spirit-filled. John 4:23-24 teaches that true worshipers will worship the Father in spirit and in truth. Worship that is Spirit-led allows us to experience God in an intimate and personal way, guiding our hearts toward surrender and transformation. Kathleen and I have learned that we are the temple of God, as 1 Corinthians 6:19-20 states, meaning that His Spirit dwells in us. This understanding deepens our worship, reminding us that it is not about external actions but about an internal connection with God.

To implement Spirit-led worship in practical ways, we invite the Holy Spirit into every aspect of our daily routine. We start our mornings with prayer, asking for guidance, wisdom, and an open heart to recognize His presence. Throughout the day, we pause to reflect on His leading, ensuring that our decisions and interactions align with His will. Spirit-led worship also means allowing spontaneous praise to flow whenever we feel compelled. If a moment of gratitude arises, we acknowledge it with worship, whether through a short prayer, a song, or simply speaking words of thanksgiving.

Spiritual worship instills a holy fear of God, as seen in Matthew 5:3 and Psalms 51:17. It also gives us powerful confidence before Him. Second Corinthians 3:12-17 affirms that through Christ, we can approach God boldly, no longer bound by fear but embraced in grace. Galatians 4:6-7 declares that we are heirs, not servants, allowing us to worship from a place of freedom rather than obligation. Worship is meant to be uninhibited, flowing from the heart with joy and reverence.

One practical way we cultivate confidence in worship is by declaring God's promises aloud. Speaking scripture over our lives reminds us of His faithfulness, reinforcing a sense of boldness in approaching Him. We also encourage our children to do the same, ensuring that they understand they are beloved and welcomed in His presence. Confidence before God is developed when we internalize His love, replacing fear with assurance.

One night I was heavy with worry, the kind of fear that grips a parent's heart when their child is suffering. It was around 2 a.m., the world outside still and quiet, but inside, our home was filled with cries—our second daughter burning with fever, her little body radiating so much heat that it felt like fire against our hands.

There was no hospital nearby, no immediate help to call upon. But there was one thing we knew to do—pray and worship.

Kathleen and I lifted our voices, not in desperation, but in declaration. We reminded God of who He is, of His promises, of the healing power spoken in His Word. We did not plead—we proclaimed. We did not panic—we praised.

And then, something shifted.

The atmosphere thickened, His presence filling the room like a holy wave. And in an instant, our daughter, still crying moments before, suddenly stilled within 10-15 minutes. Her body relaxed, her breathing softened and was knocked out. She was slain in the Spirit—completely overcome by the presence of God.

We watched in awe as the fever vanished, her temperature returning to normal, her little frame now resting in perfect peace. It was not medicine, it was not time—it was the power of God manifesting in that very moment.

It was a reminder, once again, that when His presence is near, healing follows. Miracles are not distant, nor reserved for another time, another place. They are here, now, moving among us, responding to faith, responding to worship.

Because worship is not just about singing—it is about stepping into divine alignment, calling forth the reality of heaven into the present. And in that alignment, anything is possible.

To implement unity in worship, we prioritize worshiping together as a family. Whether in church or at home, we make time to worship collectively. Singing together, reading scripture as a unit, and sharing reflections encourage a spirit of togetherness. We also extend this practice to our community, inviting friends to join in worship, reinforcing the bond of faith.

To be spiritually nourished, worship must be in accordance with the Word of God. Colossians 3:16 instructs us to let the Word dwell richly in us, ensuring that our worship aligns with biblical truth. Worship is not based on emotion or preference—it must be anchored in scripture. Deuteronomy 18:14-22 emphasizes the need for discernment, guarding against influences that contradict His truth. We prioritize biblical worship, ensuring that every song, prayer, and reflection is rooted in His Word.

A practical way we ensure scripture governs our worship is by incorporating the Word into our prayers. Rather than relying solely on our own words, we pray scripture, using passages that reflect God's promises and truth. This not only strengthens our faith but also ensures that worship remains centered on His revelation rather than fleeting emotions.

Worship must edify us, as seen in Ephesians 6:17 and Hebrews 4:12. The Word of God is alive, capable of piercing our hearts and transforming our spirits. True worship should leave us strengthened, encouraged, and aligned with His truth. Worship that lacks substance fails to feed the spirit—it becomes an empty ritual rather than a powerful encounter with God.

Worship is the lifeblood of our faith, the sacred rhythm that moves through every corner of our lives. It is not something we merely do—it is something we live. Matthew 22:37-40 calls us to love the Lord with all our heart, soul, and mind, a reminder that worship requires full engagement. It is a surrender that involves every part of us—our thoughts, emotions, creativity, and devotion. Worship is holistic, touching not only our spirits but shaping our minds and actions in profound ways.

We have learned that worship is not confined to song alone. Some days, Kathleen and I lift our voices in praise, letting music fill our home with the sound of gratitude. Other times, we sit in quiet reflection, immersing ourselves in scripture, allowing the truth of His Word to breathe life into our souls. Journaling has become a treasured practice—writing down prayers, revelations, and testimonies of God's faithfulness, capturing moments of His presence in a way that deepens our connection with Him. Creativity in worship opens doors to new encounters with God, reminding us that praise comes in many forms.

Through these principles, we have discovered that worship is not simply an act of devotion—it is the foundation upon which our faith is built. It nourishes our spirits, strengthens our bond with God, and brings clarity to His truth. Worship is the key that keeps us connected, ensuring that no matter the season, our hearts remain steadfast in Him.

More than anything, worship is personal. It is where faith meets surrender, where love meets allegiance, where we offer ourselves fully to Him. It is not about routine—it is about relationship. Ephesians 3:20-21 reminds us that God moves in ways beyond what we ask or imagine, working through us to accomplish His will. Worship is how we align ourselves with His power, allowing it to transform not only our hearts but the very steps we take each day.

For Kathleen and me, worship is not bound to time or place—it lives in our daily rhythms, shaping our conversations, guiding our decisions, and filling the spaces between the busyness of life. Worship has strengthened our home, nurtured our marriage, and become the melody that carries us forward. It is in worship that we find renewal, restoration, and the ever-present reminder that we are never alone.

Worship is meant to encompass every part of who we are—heart, mind, will, and body. It is an invitation to bring the fullness of human experience before God, allowing His presence to meet us wherever we are.

One of the most powerful aspects of worship is how it engages emotions in their entirety. Joy spills over in praise, just as Psalms 47:1-2 calls us to clap our hands and shout to God with triumph. Romans 14:17 reminds us that the kingdom of God is righteousness, peace, and joy—worship is meant to reflect this, to be an overflowing expression of love and gratitude. For Kathleen and me, worship is never mechanical; it is alive with emotion, whether through exuberant singing, deep intercession, or moments of quiet surrender.

But worship is also a place for sorrow, for grief, for the cries of the weary. The Psalms are filled with moments of lament, where David pours out his heart, unfiltered and raw before God. Psalms 22:1-2 and Lamentations 3:1-23 remind us that worship is not just about celebrating victory but also about bringing our burdens honestly before Him. We have clung to this truth in seasons of hardship, trusting that even in pain, worship remains a refuge. There have been moments when praise felt heavy, but in those moments, we found that bringing our sorrow before God did not weaken us—it strengthened us, healing our hearts in ways we couldn't have imagined.

Worship also requires the engagement of the will—it is a choice. James 5:16 speaks of confessing sins and praying for healing, and Psalms 119:35-37 calls for divine guidance. Worship is not simply an emotional experience but an act of commitment and repentance. Before we lift our voices in praise, Kathleen and I take time for reflection—examining areas where we need God's correction, where we must surrender more deeply. Worship is the space where transformation happens, where repentance leads to renewal, where we align ourselves with God's heart.

Physical expression is equally vital in worship. It is impossible to read scripture without seeing how posture—bowing, lifting hands, shouting, kneeling—plays a role in surrender and devotion. Psalms 95:6 encourages us to bow before the Lord, and Psalms 47:1 calls us to raise our hands in praise. For us, worship is never confined to words alone. We engage our bodies—whether in kneeling before Him in reverence, lifting our hands in thanksgiving, or even dancing in celebration. There is power in expressing worship physically, in using posture to symbolize surrender, gratitude, and joy.

Worship is not just an activity; it is the essence of faith. It fuels the soul, deepens our relationship with God, and keeps us connected to Him in every season of life. Whether in joy or sorrow, in quiet moments or exuberant praise, worship is the key to remaining close to Him. It is the heart's response to His goodness, the foundation of spiritual resilience, and the source of unshakable strength.

Worship is the lens through which we view life, shaping not only our faith but our interactions, perspectives, and daily rhythms. It is a continuous unfolding of gratitude, devotion, and surrender—a practice that doesn't just happen in designated moments but permeates everything we do.

One of the most important aspects of worship is the motivation behind it. Isaiah 58 warns against empty rituals, reminding us that worship must be driven by a deep, personal desire to honor God. It cannot be reduced to routine or obligation—it must be sincere. Kathleen and I consistently examine our hearts, asking whether our worship flows from love or habit. We have learned that when worship becomes about performance, it loses its power. When it remains rooted in genuine devotion, it transforms everything.

Practically applying this principle has deepened our experience of worship, allowing it to breathe life into our relationship with God. Worship is not simply an act—it is our identity in Christ. It keeps our faith vibrant, renews our spirits, and reminds us of the depth of God's truth.

Worship is also meant to touch every part of our lives, influencing how we love, serve, and extend grace to others. It shapes how we respond to challenges, how we celebrate victories, and how we commit to justice and mercy. Over the years, we have discovered that worship is never confined to church—it happens in our daily interactions, in the decisions we make, and in the quiet moments when we pause to reflect on His goodness.

Ephesians 3:20-21 reminds us that God's power works within us, allowing us to glorify Him beyond what we could ever ask or imagine. Worship is the natural response to that truth—a continuous declaration of His greatness. For Kathleen and me, worship doesn't end when we step away from a gathering; it follows us into our daily lives, shaping how we manage our time, our resources, and our relationships.

Kathleen and I often find moments of worship in nature, pausing to acknowledge the intricate beauty of His work. There is something humbling about standing under the vast sky, walking among the trees, hearing the steady rhythm of the ocean—it is a reminder that all of creation sings His praise, and we are invited to join in that chorus.

Worship is also rooted in gratitude. Psalms 104 and 145 teach that God sustains life, providing for all of creation. Recognizing His provision is an essential part of our worship. We make it a habit to express gratitude daily—not just for grand blessings but for the simplest gifts. A meal shared, a door opened, a need met—these, too, are moments of worship, reminders that His hand is always at work.

More than anything, worship is a relationship. It is the quiet conversation between the Creator and His children, the place where love meets devotion, where surrender meets peace. Worship is not just something we do—it is how we live.

Worship has always been a central thread in my life. Before I encountered Jesus, before I knew His healing power, worship was already deeply ingrained in me. Growing up in a Hindu family, it was an integral part of our daily routine—an expression of reverence taught from a young age, embedded in the songs we sang and the prayers we recited.

I remember the rituals vividly—worshipping the sun god in the early hours of the morning, pouring milk onto the earth while chanting prayers. There was devotion, there was faith, but it was directed toward things made by human hands. Everything was a god—the sun, fire, the earth—tangible objects that could be seen and touched. Worship was deeply emotional, an experience that could stir the heart, but it did not bring the presence of a living God.

There were manifestations, moments that seemed supernatural—people possessed as drums beat and sacrifices were made. I recall being taken to a temple where milk and honey appeared to flow from images of Hindu gods and goddesses. My mother led me there, eager to show me these miracles. Thousands came, believing, placing money before these images, convinced that they had witnessed something divine. Yet, only the owner of the house ever truly saw these wonders. The belief was strong because worship was powerful, and when people experience something beyond the ordinary, their faith deepens—regardless of where it is placed.

But then came the encounter that changed everything. At 14, Jesus healed me, and suddenly, worship was no longer about images, rituals, or man-made offerings. It became something living, something real. I stepped into the presence of the God of creation—not carved from stone, not painted on temple walls, but alive, speaking, moving, transforming. Worship was no longer an act of repetition—it became communion, an experience of being held in the presence of the One who created all things.

This is why I love worshipping Jesus, why I press in until I step into the Holy of Holies. Worship is not just something I do—it is a place I enter, a space where I know He is near. And most of my friends who have been there, those who have stepped into that depth of worship, I connect with them in a way that is almost beyond words. I feel like they are my blood brothers, bound by the same hunger, the same pursuit of His presence. Worship leaders—those who have entered that sacred space—I feel an immediate connection with them because they understand what it means to dwell there, to live in that place, to never be satisfied with anything less.

True worship is more than emotion—it is encounter. It is knowing Him, feeling His presence, seeing His hand through signs, wonders, and miracles. It is stepping beyond what can be explained and entering into what can only be experienced. And once you have been there, once you have felt the weight of His glory, nothing else compares.

Worship is the thread that connects us not only to God but to one another, leading us to rejoice in the future glory of His people. It is the bridge between the present and eternity—a promise that His kingdom will be fully realized. Each time we worship, we are reminded that we are part of something greater than ourselves, something everlasting. Worship stirs hope within us, igniting faith that is unwavering, resilient, and full of anticipation.

It is impossible to separate worship from life itself. The Psalms reveal this beautifully, illustrating how worship flows through every human experience—joy, sorrow, triumph, and struggle. Worship is not just reserved for moments in church; it is meant to be carried into the everyday. It shapes prayer, strengthens spiritual armor, and becomes the space where we bring the concerns of the world before God. Worship shifts perspectives—it teaches us to see life through the lens of faith,

THE HEARTBEAT OF HEAVEN

reminding us that God is sovereign over all things. In times of uncertainty, we have witnessed firsthand how worship transforms attitudes, lifting burdens, restoring peace, and reinforcing trust in Him.

But worship is never meant to exist in isolation. First Corinthians 1:2 reminds us that worship is most powerful when shared among the people of God. Though we come from different backgrounds, different experiences, we are one body in Christ, as First Corinthians 12:12-13 and Ephesians 4:1-6 affirm. Worship unites us, reminding us that faith transcends differences, that we are called to stand together, lifting our voices in praise. There is something sacred about corporate worship—something deeply enriching and strengthening. Gathering with others, lifting songs of adoration in unity, is not just an act of faith but an embodiment of community, a glimpse of what heaven will be like.

For Kathleen and me, worship has been the anchor in every season, the force that keeps us steady and aligned with God's heart. It is where we find refuge, where we draw strength, and where we remain connected not only to Him but to those walking this journey alongside us. Worship is not simply a moment—it is a movement, a calling, a way of life that carries us forward toward the fulfillment of God's promises.

Worship is the heartbeat of our faith, the sacred thread that weaves through every aspect of life, drawing us closer to God with each moment. It is not confined to songs or services—it is a way of living, a continual offering of devotion, trust, and surrender.

We have learned that worship must not be compartmentalized but fully embraced, shaping our thoughts, guiding our decisions, and strengthening our relationship with God. It is not something we step into and out of—it surrounds us, anchors us, and becomes the rhythm by which we walk in faith. Worship reminds us that we are part of something greater than ourselves, invited to lift our hearts in praise, both individually and in the community of believers.

We have seen how worship flourishes when approached as a communal experience. First Corinthians 12:26 teaches us that worship binds believers together—it is where joy is shared, burdens are carried, and faith is strengthened. It is not about standing alone but about walking together, lifting one another up, and allowing worship to become a refuge for all. We have witnessed the beauty of worship when people are empowered to use their God-given gifts—whether through music, prayer, teaching, or service. Every act of worship is an offering, a sacred expression of devotion to God.

Worship moves in two directions—vertically toward God and horizontally toward His people. Revelation 4 and 5 paint a picture of worship in heaven, where praises rise before His throne and unity is perfected among believers. We have come to understand that worship must reflect this balance—honoring God while fostering connection among His people. It strengthens relationships, deepens faith, and reminds us that we are never alone in this journey.

True worship is not passive—it is active, engaging every part of our being. The Psalms show us the depth of expressive worship—through music, prayer, lament, and celebration. Worship is not simply an intellectual exercise but a transformational experience that moves through body, mind, and spirit.

Kathleen and I have found that the essence of true worship is not confined to a single act or moment. It is expressed through conversations, choices, and faith-filled actions. It is carried through the day, woven into every interaction, shaping every aspect of life. Worship is our foundation, our refuge, our source of renewal.

And as we continue this journey, we remain committed to honouring Him with all that we are—seeking His presence, embracing His truth, and ensuring that our worship remains authentic, biblical, and transformative. Because worship is not just what we do—it is who we are.

PRAISING HIM IN THE STORM

When couples face hardships—whether through loss, misunderstandings, financial struggles, or deep emotional pain—there is a natural temptation to withdraw from each other and even from God. Kathleen and I have walked through some of the darkest valleys imaginable, moments where our faith was tested beyond measure. In those moments, we encountered the common errors many couples make—errors that do not just damage a marriage but disrupt a person's connection with God.

Losing Tihomir a good friend was like losing a piece of my soul, a wound so deep that time couldn't simply erase it. We had shared everything—prayer, ministry, dreams for the future. He was my brother in Christ, my Jonathan, and I was his David. Every morning at 5 a.m., before the world woke up, we would pray together, believing that no matter how dark the war around us got, God was still moving. He translated for me, helped baptize people, supported Kathleen and the children, carried an unshakable passion for Jesus, and was determined to become a lawyer to fight for justice.

Then, in one unbearable moment, he was gone.

I remember the seconds after hearing the news—everything around me faded into silence, a heaviness pressing against my chest, stealing the breath from my lungs. My mind struggled to process the words. Dead? *How?* I had just been heading to meet him. Five minutes earlier, and we would have been together. Five minutes—the cruel divide between life and loss.

Grief is not just sadness; it's an unraveling. My faith, which had carried me through wars and uncertainty, suddenly felt shaken. How could God allow this? *Why him? Why now?* I had seen miracles, witnessed transformation, stood in places where heaven felt closer than ever. But in this moment, all I could see was emptiness.

My police officer friend warned me not to attend the funeral. People wanted me dead, and going could have been a death sentence. It felt like another cruel twist—unable to mourn, unable to say goodbye, unable to honor the life of the man who had stood by my side through everything. How do you grieve when you're forced to pretend it never happened? I stayed away. And in doing so, I felt like I had lost everything—not only my closest friend but my right to mourn him publicly. The bitterness crept in. I stopped entering God's presence the way I once did, stopped pushing into the Holy of Holies where my spirit would be consumed by His glory. I continued to preach, but it lacked depth. I carried the weight of grief, but I did not surrender it in worship.

For over twenty-six years, I wrestled with grief, never fully finding closure until I stood in his hometown at a gravesite, saying my goodbyes with my son. But in those early days, I did not handle my sorrow the way I should have. My error, the error many of us make, was thinking that if I stopped talking to God, I would teach Him a lesson. It was a childish notion—that ignoring Him would somehow make Him feel my pain more deeply, that my silence would force Him to explain why He allowed Tihomir to die. But God does not operate under human emotions; He does not need reminders of our suffering, because He already knows.

AS FOR ME AND MY SPOUSE WE WILL PRAISE THE LORD

By October of 2006, Kathleen had gone to Canada to give birth to our fourth baby, and I remained behind. It was a quiet, lonely morning, about 10 a.m., after I had dropped my daughters off at Montessori school. I sat in the living room, grieving, sad, discouraged, refusing to pray, refusing to enter worship. Then something happened—the Holy Spirit entered the room. It was only the second time in my life that I heard His voice audibly.

I did something I regretted until I got myself on track. I shut God out. The worship I once carried like breath itself became silent. I still preached, I still spoke about faith, but I avoided the deep places—the Holy of Holies where I had once felt consumed by His presence. I didn't want to enter His presence, because I was afraid. Afraid that if I truly opened my heart, I would collapse under the weight of my grief.

Months passed. Kathleen had gone back to Canada to have our fourth baby. I was alone, left with my thoughts, and I knew—*I couldn't keep running.*

Then came the morning when everything changed.

It was 10 a.m., an ordinary day, yet the pain was unbearable. After dropping my daughters off at Montessori school, I walked into the house, sat in the living room, and let the weight of sorrow crush me. I was tired of being strong. Tired of carrying my anger. Tired of pretending that I wasn't furious at God for not intervening.

And then, the atmosphere shifted.

I didn't just feel the Holy Spirit enter the room—I *heard* Him. His voice filled the space, audible, undeniable, as if He had been waiting for this moment all along.

"Can you put these pieces together?"

I saw my life—a shattered glass, broken beyond repair, scattered across the ground. The answer was clear. *"No,"* I whispered.

Then came the words that unraveled me.

"Let me help you put it together."

It wasn't a command. It wasn't forceful. It was an invitation, drenched in love, filled with compassion, wrapped in peace. Suddenly, I felt arms I could not see surrounding me, holding me in a way no human could. Grief and comfort intertwined, the weight of sorrow met by the presence of restoration.

I cried—not just because I missed Tihomir, but because I had spent months trying to punish God with silence, thinking I could shut Him out when all He wanted was to heal me. My prayers had been shallow, my worship hesitant, because I was afraid of going deep. But there, in that living room, I surrendered. I let go of the bitterness. And as I did, I realized something—God had never given up on me. Not even when I tried to turn away. Not even when I refused to speak to Him.

Since that day, I have avoided the common error of running from God when pain strikes. I may never understand why bad things happen, why prayers seem unanswered, why some losses remain unexplainable. But I do know this—praise is the bridge between despair and healing. Worship is not just for the easy seasons; it is for the moments when sorrow makes breathing difficult.

Kathleen and I have carried this truth through every storm. We have lost three grandchildren to miscarriage, moments that could have broken us, but they did not. Because we have learned—God is always watching, always working, always noting the attacks of the enemy. And He will reward faithfulness.

So we praise Him. Not because life is perfect. But because even in grief, even in confusion, even when we don't understand, He is still worthy. And when we worship, we step into a love deeper than pain itself.

Praise is foundational in our marriage, shaping how we connect with God and each other. It is not just a practice we engage in—it is a lifestyle that strengthens our faith, deepens our relationship, and creates a sacred atmosphere in our home. Psalm 117 reminds us to praise the Lord, acknowledging His enduring love and faithfulness. Worship in marriage is an intentional choice, and structuring it properly can prevent common errors that couples often face.

One of the most frequent misunderstandings in implementing praise and worship as a couple is the belief that both partners must know the same songs, sing together, or even like the same worship music. In reality, praise is deeply personal and operates powerfully in the spiritual realm regardless of individual musical preferences. We have learned that worship is not about uniformity—it is about authenticity. During our private devotions, we each choose songs that resonate with us individually, allowing them to minister to our hearts. Some songs bring me to my knees, overwhelming me with God's presence, while Kathleen has her own selections that uplift her spirit. When we come together for morning coffee and devotions, we intentionally play worship music that creates an atmosphere of unity and reverence without forcing ourselves into a single mold.

One common mistake couples make is condescension or arrogance in praising the Lord. This happens when one spouse assumes their way of praise is more spiritual or correct than the other's. True praise must be filled with humility, respecting each other's choices. We have cultivated an environment where both of us have the freedom to express praise in ways that feel natural to us, whether it is through song, scripture reading, or quiet reflection.

Another error is approaching praise too stiffly, formally, or coldly, which diminishes intimacy with God. Praise with worship should be filled with joy, surrender, and engagement, reflecting the warmth of God's presence. When praise and worship feel like an obligation rather than a heartfelt connection, it can create distance between spouses and their spiritual experience. We ensure that worship in our marriage is free and organic, allowing moments of spontaneous praise and prayer without rigidity.

Some couples struggle with praise being too casual, treating it as an afterthought rather than a sacred act. While praise does not require a structured format, it should be approached with reverence. Hebrews 12:28 reminds us that praise with worship must reflect the majesty of God. In our marriage, we balance spontaneity with intentionality, ensuring that we do not take worship lightly but embrace it as a meaningful encounter with God.

Needless repetition in praise—whether in song or words—can cause people to disengage mentally. While repetition has its place in worship, excessive use can make it mechanical rather than heartfelt. We avoid this by introducing variety in our praise, ensuring that our praise remains fresh and impactful. Whether through different songs, new scripture readings, or changing how we pray, we keep worship dynamic and engaging.

A lack of preparation can hinder the effectiveness of praise in marriage. While spontaneous praise is beautiful, structure allows it to be a regular practice rather than something that happens sporadically. We ensure that we make time for praise, scheduling moments for prayer and devotion rather than hoping they happen naturally. This preparation fosters deeper engagement, making our worship intentional and fulfilling.

Loss of spontaneity is another challenge couples face. While preparation is necessary, praise should also include moments where the Holy Spirit leads. The confidence that comes from good preparation allows for freedom in praise, making space for God's presence to move unexpectedly. We embrace spontaneity by leaving room for praise with worship beyond scheduled times. If a song speaks to us unexpectedly, if a prayer flows from a conversation, or if God prompts us toward an act of devotion, we respond freely.

Addressing these common errors has strengthened praise in our marriage, allowing it to be an integral part of our lives rather than an occasional act. Worship transforms relationships by aligning hearts with God, reinforcing love and unity. It is not about perfection or identical practices—it is about creating an atmosphere where praise and adoration flow naturally between spouses. Kathleen and I are committed to ensuring that praise remains the heartbeat of our marriage, guiding us spiritually and emotionally through every season.

Storms come when we least expect them—interrupting our joy, testing our faith, and shaking our foundation. Some arrive as small gusts, brief moments of hardship, while others rage on, leaving devastation in their wake. But through every storm, Kathleen and I have learned one truth: we will praise the Lord.

One of the hardest tempests we faced was the loss of our first grandchild. When our daughter shared the news of her pregnancy, she radiated joy. As the first of our children to marry and the first to step into motherhood, her excitement was shared by the entire family. We embraced the dream of holding our grandchild, witnessing new life unfold before us. But then, five months later, that dream shattered. The miscarriage felt like a violent wind, sweeping away our hopes, leaving sorrow in its place.

We grieved deeply. Tears flowed. Questions arose. We wondered why, especially knowing we were covered by the protection of Jesus. And yet, in the depths of our pain, we had no choice but to turn to Him. Even when we were angry, even when we doubted, even when praise felt like the hardest thing to do—He remained.

I often thought back to my daughter's early faith. She was just two years old when, while we were in Croatia, she waited all day as I was out in the city to tell me, *"Jesus kissed me and told me He is coming back.*" When I asked how she knew it was Him, she giggled and said, "*He was dressed in white, and I just know, Dad—you silly guy.*" That unwavering trust had carried her through mission trips, speaking engagements, and life's highs and lows. And now, we too needed to lean on faith—to praise God, even through this storm. And in time, we saw His faithfulness unfold. She went on to have two beautiful daughters, reminders of His mercy and grace.

But life, in its unpredictable nature, brought more storms. Years later, another one of our children came to us with excitement—they were expecting! Around the same time, another child, already eleven weeks pregnant, shared the same wonderful news. Two new lives, two joys on the horizon. Then, yet again, sorrow arrived. Both miscarried.

It was crushing. We had already endured this loss once—how could it happen again? Pain engulfed us, sweeping through our family like a raging tide. We wept together, held each other, whispered prayers between sobs. And yet, through it all, one thing remained unchanged: God.

Praising Him did not come easily. I was furious. I had been born again in 1983, and from that moment, I felt spoiled by His blessings. I was used to God answering, used to His favor surrounding me. So why now? Why this? And so, I told Him exactly how I felt. I didn't hold back my frustration, my hurt, my anger. And yet, despite my emotions, He did not reject me. He did not yell back. He embraced me, wrapped me in His peace, and reminded me that He was still present.

It's not always easy to see the good in life's painful moments. But even in the storm, we choose to praise Him. Not because the hardship disappears, but because praise anchors our hearts in His truth. It builds resilience, strengthens faith, and keeps us moving forward. We may not understand now, but He sees tomorrow. And so, Kathleen and I, along with our children, will continue to praise the Lord—through every season, through every storm.

SILENT HEARTS

The absence of praise in a marriage creates a spiritual void that leaves a couple vulnerable to many destructive forces. Praise is not just about singing or praying—it is about inviting God's presence into the relationship, allowing Him to shape the foundation of love, trust, and commitment. When praise is missing, that foundation weakens, making space for struggles that can lead to emotional distance, breakdowns in communication, and, ultimately, separation.

One of the most devastating consequences of a lack of praise is the rise of temptations like infidelity. When couples neglect praise, they lose sight of God's design for marriage—faithfulness, intimacy, and spiritual unity. Without the anchor of praise, emotional disconnection sets in, making spouses more susceptible to seeking validation or connection outside their marriage. Praise reminds couples that love is built on God's presence, but when it is absent, selfish desires and external temptations can take root.

Addictions often creep into marriages where praise is neglected. Alcohol, drugs, pornography, food, excessive spending—all of these can become coping mechanisms when a couple does not turn to God in times of stress, loneliness, or emotional pain. Praise is a weapon against these strongholds, helping couples refocus their dependence on God instead of temporary fixes. Without worship, people seek escape in harmful habits rather than finding peace in God's presence.

A lack of commitment is another destructive force in relationships. Praise teaches surrender, sacrifice, and patience—qualities that strengthen commitment in marriage. Without praise, frustration replaces endurance, leading couples to question whether their relationship is worth fighting for. Worship reinforces the sacred nature of marriage, reminding spouses that their union is not just an agreement between two people but a covenant with God.

Worry and fear thrive in relationships where praise is missing. Without praise, couples carry burdens alone rather than surrendering them to God. Anxiety about finances, family struggles, or personal insecurities grows unchecked, leading to tension and conflict. Praise shifts focus from uncertainty to trust, but when it is absent, doubt takes control, making even small issues feel insurmountable.

A marriage without praise often lacks motivation and vision. Praise awakens purpose, reminding couples of the bigger picture—God's calling for their lives together. Without it, relationships can become stagnant, with couples feeling stuck in routine, lacking direction, and failing to support each other's growth. Praise brings renewal, fresh perspective, and the strength to move forward, but when it is missing, relationships can feel aimless.

The absence of praise is not just a minor issue—it is a gateway to marital destruction. Kathleen and I have seen firsthand how praise strengthens love, breaks cycles of frustration, and shields against external pressures. When God is absent from a relationship, struggles intensify, but when praise is present, love deepens, faith grows, and the marriage stands strong against any attack.

When we learn to praise God, something profound happens—not just in our spiritual lives, but in the way we see and interact with others, especially our spouse. Praise shifts our perspective, teaching us to focus

AS FOR ME AND MY SPOUSE WE WILL PRAISE THE LORD

on God's goodness rather than life's imperfections. This mindset extends into our relationships, making it easier to appreciate, uplift, and encourage rather than criticize, doubt, or dwell on regrets. We have seen this firsthand in our marriage.

Praise is powerful because it trains us to look for the good. When we consistently praise God, we are reminded that He is always working, always faithful, and always bringing beauty out of brokenness. This same principle applies to how we view our spouse. Instead of focusing on their flaws, mistakes, or weaknesses, we begin to see their potential, their strengths, and the ways God is shaping them. Just as we learn to trust that God is moving in our lives, we also learn to trust His work in our partner, making it easier to extend grace and patience.

Kathleen and I have experienced moments when frustration could have led to negativity—times when we could have dwelled on past mistakes or shortcomings. But when praise is present in our lives, it shifts the atmosphere. Instead of criticizing, we find ourselves offering words of encouragement, compliments, and gratitude. Praise softens our hearts, reminding us that love is built on support, not judgment.

Choosing to praise God regularly makes optimism a natural mindset. When we praise, we focus on blessings, rather than disappointments, and that perspective carries into how we treat each other. We have noticed that when praise is woven into our daily lives, joy and encouragement overflow into our relationship. We start celebrating small victories, appreciating everyday moments, and speaking life into each other's dreams and ambitions.

Praise also eliminates the weight of past regrets. Many couples struggle with looking back, feeling the sting of bad decisions or missed opportunities. But praise reminds us that God is a God of restoration. When we praise, we proclaim His ability to redeem and renew, allowing that truth to shape how we view our spouse. Instead of holding onto mistakes, we embrace growth, knowing that every trial has brought us closer to where God wants us to be.

We have committed to living with a heart of praise because we have seen its impact—not just spiritually, but emotionally and relationally. Praise fills our home with peace, strengthens our bond, and keeps us looking forward instead of backward. A marriage rooted in praise is a marriage filled with encouragement, joy, and unwavering support.

There are moments in life when sorrow quietly settles into the heart, unnoticed by the world, but deeply felt within the soul. The ache doesn't always come with loud cries or visible grief—it lingers in the silence, hidden behind smiles and daily routines. For Kathleen and me, one of those moments arrived when our son got married and chose to move to Australia.

His marriage came sooner than I had anticipated, and though I was happy for him, I felt an unexpected emptiness. Just a year before, I was walking beside him through university, sharing conversations, dreams, and laughter. We had built a bond, and now, in what felt like the blink of an eye, he was gone, I was replaced—starting a life of his own, far away. I knew I should have been celebrating this new chapter in his life, but my heart was heavy with the feeling of loss.

Instead of staying home for a painful goodbye when he decided to leave for Australia, Kathleen and I traveled to Israel. It was easier that way, easier to avoid standing at the door watching him leave. But even as we flew across the world, he found a way to remind us of his love. On the plane we read letters we found when we opened our passports and discovered he had tucked inside—words filled with warmth and gratitude. He spoke of how much he loved us, how he admired the way I prayed in my office, how he longed to be like us and hope his marriage will follow in our steps. His words were a gift, yet my soul remained unsettled.

AS FOR ME AND MY SPOUSE WE WILL PRAISE THE LORD

I wrestled with my emotions, torn between my personal sorrow and the understanding that this was his dream. When we spoke, I encouraged him to live his life fully. After all, I had done the same. At eighteen, I left home to migrate to Canada, working on a tobacco farm, learning humility, gaining experience and wisdom. Leaving home was painful then, and I knew it would be painful now—both for him and for me. It felt like a lesson coming full circle, a taste of my own medicine.

Years later, I learned my mother cried for over three years after I left. I never knew how much she had grieved until she told me, and by then, time had slipped away. It reminded me that no matter how much we love, we cannot recover lost years. But as we grow older, we learn to cherish the ones who raised us, to appreciate the sacrifices they made, to understand their quiet sorrows.

I fell into a deep depression. It was like sinking into a darkness I couldn't escape. I cried often, mourning the distance, feeling like I was in a hole with no way out. And yet, through my grief, I held onto one truth—I was proud of him. I knew that maturity, growth, and wisdom come through responsibility and independence. He was stepping into his own journey, and I wanted to support him, even though Kathleen and I had silent hearts.

In the midst of my depression, I heard the Holy Spirit whisper: *Jump up and praise the Lord.* At first, it took effort, strength I wasn't sure I had. Kathleen and I chose to praise the Lord anyway, declaring His faithfulness even when our emotions felt heavy. We knew that God was in control, even when our hearts were aching.

The hardest moments were the family gatherings—birthdays, holidays, celebrations where his absence felt like an empty chair at the table. But as the year passed, something miraculous happened. One day, he called and told us he was moving back to Canada with his wife. The joy that flooded my heart was overwhelming, an overdose of happiness, a light returning after months of silence. Not only did we get our son back, but we gained a daughter.

For a long time, my heart had been quiet, wounded in a way that was invisible to others. I had smiled through the pain, carried my sorrow privately, but God had seen it all. And in His goodness, He reminded me that He takes note of our silent heartaches, our hidden grief. He sees the tears we don't show, hears the prayers we whisper in solitude. And He rewards us.

Through every storm—through sadness, separation, and waiting—Kathleen and I have learned one thing: *We will praise the Lord.* Not just when life is easy, but even when the heart is silent, even when joy feels distant. Because He is always working, always comforting, always guiding. And even in moments of quiet sorrow, He never fails.

UNLEASHING HEAVEN'S POWER

Before I met Kathleen, praise and worship was already shaping my life in ways I never could have imagined. It was what I felt unleashed heaven's power—where the presence of God became so strong at times that I could barely stand during my time with the Lord. It was more than just singing or praying—it was an encounter, a force that unlocked the supernatural, deepened my relationship with God, and transformed me from the inside out. Worship became my identity, my connection to God's voice, the very thing that branded me with His presence.

I remember the moment when praise first led me into an experience that was beyond human explanation. I was just seventeen years old, newly filled with the Holy Spirit, navigating the depths of faith in a way that felt raw and uncontainable. Praise was my lifeline, the place where I found clarity, strength, and an undeniable connection to God.

One Sunday evening after church, I was sitting in my bedroom behind the door that connected to the kitchen. The house was quiet, and I thought we had company because I kept hearing someone calling my name. It wasn't just once—it happened two or three times, distinct, clear, as though someone was standing nearby.

I stepped into the kitchen and asked my mother who was calling me. She looked at me with confusion. *No one is here,* she said. *Just your dad, and he hasn't called you.* That answer should have settled things, but it didn't. The voice had been real—I knew what I had heard.

I went back to my room and continued reading my Bible, flipping through the pages of Malachi, when something incredible happened. For the first time, I heard the audible voice of God. It wasn't just a feeling or an impression—it was as if someone was physically speaking the words to me, guiding me, asking me to write. My hands shook as I scribbled down what I was hearing, realizing that I was receiving my first sermon, not by my own wisdom but by the Holy Spirit Himself.

The scripture was Malachi 4:1-3:

"For behold, the day is coming, burning like an oven, and all the proud, yes, all who do wickedly will be stubble. And the day which is coming shall burn them up," says the Lord of hosts, "That will leave them neither root nor branch. But to you who fear My name, the Sun of Righteousness shall arise with healing in His wings; and you shall go out and grow fat like stall-fed calves. You shall trample the wicked, for they shall be ashes under the soles of your feet on the day that I do this," says the Lord of hosts.

The weight of the words sat heavy in my chest. It was powerful, direct, filled with the heart of God. But fear crept in. *Was this truly meant for me?* I told God, *If this is my message, it is a great sermon. But if it is meant for your people, You need to tell the pastor to ask me.* I was shy, anxious, filled with social phobia, unable to speak comfortably in front of others. The idea of standing on a platform and delivering a sermon seemed impossible.

The next day, I went to church for a men's meeting. And then, out of nowhere, the pastor called my name. *"Can you share a word with us this Thursday?"* My heart stopped. God had answered.

Thursday came quickly, and with it, my nerves. The service started, and all the pastors, including me, sat on stage, facing the 200 people in attendance. I stared at the crowd, feeling the weight of expectation pressing against me. The fear was suffocating. I whispered to God, *I cannot do this.* And in the midst of my panic, His voice came again, steady, unwavering. *"When you cannot do it, that's when I can do it through you."*

I stood on the platform, trembling, gripping my notes, and then something supernatural happened. The sermon lifted off the paper as if it was alive, flowing effortlessly from my mouth. Words I hadn't rehearsed, boldness I had never known—it wasn't me speaking anymore. It was the Holy Spirit.

Within fifteen minutes, people began coming forward, crying as the presence of God intensified in the room. It was the first time I saw people falling under the power of God. The pastor took my hands and placed them on the people, and more and more came forward. Worship had opened the heavens, making room for a movement of the Spirit that I could have never orchestrated on my own.

That night marked the beginning of something greater. Boldness began to fill me. Praise prepared my heart for the supernatural, for signs and wonders, for miracles that I had only read about in scripture. At eighteen years old, I was asked to be a pastor, and soon after, I transitioned to Canada. Praise had shaped my calling—it had positioned me in places I never thought I would be.

From that moment forward, I understood the importance of praise. It is not just about songs or melodies—it is about preparing the heart for God's presence. Praise is the act of thanking Him for what He has done, and worship is the act of inviting Him in. When you have been branded by praising God with worship, the presence of God marks you, you are changed forever.

Today, most of my closest pastor friends are worshippers, they praise God with their worship. Many of them have led worship and have learned the power of praising God before stepping into leadership roles. They have been marked by God, chosen to usher in His presence, to create space where heaven touches earth. Praise is more than a practice—it is the gateway to encounters that shape destinies.

There is no doubt in my mind— praising God with your worship is the foundation of faith. It is the invitation for God to move, the space where His presence becomes so thick it can be felt like the air itself. I have seen demons manifest and people set free. I have witnessed healing unfold in the midst of praise where it unleashed heaven's power. I have felt the tangible glory of God pressing into rooms, changing lives, breaking chains. Praise is where the supernatural collides with the natural, where heaven touches earth.

And once you have experienced it, once you have been *branded* by praising God with your worship, you are changed for a lifetime. Praise is not something you do—it is something you live.

Praise has always been central to our relationship with God. Kathleen and I have seen firsthand how structuring praising God with our worship in our lives. It transforms not only our faith but also the foundation of our marriage. The Bible provides a rich and compelling narrative of praise and worship, showing how it has been woven into the human experience since the very beginning.

Psalm 95:1-5 calls us to sing for joy to the Lord, to extol Him with thanksgiving, music, and song. It speaks to the heart of praise—recognizing God as the great King over all creation, acknowledging His sovereignty, and responding with reverence. Praise, as seen throughout Scripture, is not a one-time event but a lifestyle, a practice that connects us with God and His divine purpose.

In the Garden of Eden, praise was unbroken fellowship with God. Before sin entered the world, Adam and Eve lived in constant communion with Him, walking in His presence. Praising God with worship in the garden was sacramental—it was reflected in the Tree of Life and the Tree of the Knowledge of Good and Evil. This sets the pattern for all praise and worship in Scripture, both in humanity's fallen state and in the kingdom to come. Kathleen and I have come to recognize that praise mirrors this pattern, reminding us that even in a broken world, our praise connects us to God in a profound way.

Sacraments serve as visible words that express the reality of our fellowship with God. The practice of communion, for example, is a sacrament that reflects Christ's sacrifice, a reminder of the covering God provided for Adam and Eve's shame after their rebellion. Praise today, just as it was in Eden, is not meant to be a concession to spiritual weakness—it is a gift from God, building up faith and reaffirming our connection to Him.

Following humanity's fall, Adam and Eve were barred from God's presence. Cherubim guarded the way to the Tree of Life, crying "Holy" in reverence to God's holiness. Isaiah 6 illustrates this same truth—God's holiness is so overwhelming that sinful man cannot approach Him apart from grace. This is something Kathleen and I have deeply considered in our praise. True praise acknowledges both the holiness of God and our own inadequacy. It is not casual—it is a response to the truth that He is righteous, and we are only made acceptable through His grace.

Yet, even in humanity's brokenness, God always takes the first step. In Genesis, God sought out Adam and Eve after their rebellion, just as He continues to seek out mankind today. Isaiah 59:1-2 reminds us that God initiates praise—He calls us to Himself. We structure our praise around this truth, recognizing that worship is not something we do on our own terms but rather a response to God's invitation.

When God's presence comes, it reveals the depth of our need for Him. Adam and Eve tried to hide from God because His holiness exposed their guilt. Every revelation of God in scripture is a revelation of both His holiness and His mercy. Praise and Worship is never just about singing—it is about coming face to face with God and recognizing that His love and mercy are beyond our understanding. We have seen how confession is always the result of meeting with God. When we praise with our worship, we acknowledge both our frailty and His majesty, allowing His mercy to wash over us.

God provided a covering for Adam and Eve's shame, sacrificing the first animal to cover them. This points to the principle that praise and worship requires repentance. Without the shedding of blood, there is no forgiveness—and without repentance, true worship cannot take place. We integrate this understanding into our praise, ensuring that worship is always preceded by a moment of surrender before God. The presence of God is overwhelming, and confession naturally follows when we stand before Him.

Faith is necessary for praise and worship, as demonstrated in Genesis 4 and Hebrews 11:4. Cain and Abel both brought offerings to God, but Abel's was accepted because it was given in faith. Praise is not just about the act—it is about the heart behind it. Faith is the knowledge that God exists and the confidence that He rewards those who seek Him. Praise is not about earning God's favour but about trusting His promises. We recognize that praise must come from faith, not obligation.

Abel gave God the best of his possessions, showing that praising Him with our worship is meant to be a sacrifice of our very best. Worship offered out of duty rather than love is unacceptable to God. Hosea 6:6 reveals that God desires obedience from the heart rather than empty rituals. Praise is about giving our whole selves to Him, holding nothing back. We have embraced this principle by ensuring that our praise is not just an occasional act but a way of life—an ongoing surrender that reflects our love and devotion.

AS FOR ME AND MY SPOUSE WE WILL PRAISE THE LORD

Ultimately, praise is God-centered. Man focuses on the gift, but God focuses on the giver. He desires our hearts, not just our actions. Kathleen and I structure our praise to reflect this truth, ensuring that our praise is not simply about the music or the words but about a genuine connection with Him.

As we continue to grow in faith, we recognize that praise and worship is not a formula—it is a relationship. It is the expression of trust, surrender, and awe before God. Whether in personal devotion or communal praise, worship is the heartbeat of our spiritual journey, guiding us in grace and anchoring us in the truth of His love.

Praise is not just an act of devotion; it is a response to God's deliverance and a reflection of our faith. We have come to understand that praise must be deeply woven into our lives, shaping our relationship and guiding us in times of uncertainty. The story of Noah reveals the significance of praise, showing how it serves as a means of gratitude, intercession, and blessing.

When Noah built an altar after the flood, he demonstrated a fundamental truth— praise and worship is the response to God's salvation. Praise is never one-sided; it is a dialogue between God and His people. He calls us to Himself, and we respond in praise and thanksgiving. We have embraced this principle, ensuring that our praise is not just routine but a heartfelt expression of gratitude for all that God has done.

Noah's offering of sacrifices reflects the biblical pattern of substitution, where blood is shed in place of judgment. Praise and worship carries this same principle—acknowledging the price that was paid for our redemption. When we praise, we acknowledge Christ's sacrifice, recognizing that without His blood, we would have no access to God. We have structured our worship with this understanding, grounding our praise in the truth of Christ's work on the cross.

Noah's sacrifice involved clean animals, highlighting that worship must be done God's way, not according to personal preference. Being set apart in life is reflected in the nature of this sacrifice, demonstrating that praise must align with God's will. We have seen how structuring worship in our relationship brings unity, ensuring that we honour God in the way He desires rather than shaping praise to fit convenience.

The priesthood of Noah illustrates the power of intercession. God had every reason to destroy the earth, even after the flood, yet Noah's praise and worship stood in the gap between judgment and mercy. Praise serves as a form of spiritual intercession, preventing destruction and inviting God's blessing. We recognize that when we praise together, we are not only drawing closer to God but also standing in prayer for our family, our community, and the world.

God's response to Noah's praise and worship was a promise of blessing, showing that praise is not limited to personal devotion but has global implications. Praise is priestly in nature, bringing blessings and staying judgment. Kathleen and I have found that consistent praise in our marriage invites peace, strengthens our faith, and keeps our home aligned with God's presence.

We have integrated praise into our relationship not as an obligation but as a natural reflection of our love for God. When we praise, we are reminded that His blessings flow freely, rewarding those who seek Him with genuine hearts.

In our relationship, praise is more than an act—it is a foundation that shapes our communication, unity, and purpose. It is a daily practice, a means of drawing near to God and to one another. As we continue to implement praise in our lives, we hold onto the example of Noah, recognizing that praise and worship is both a response to deliverance and a powerful act of faith that transforms everything around us.

Praise has always been a defining aspect of faith, shaping not only personal devotion but also the structure of our homes and relationships.

AS FOR ME AND MY SPOUSE WE WILL PRAISE THE LORD

We have found that worship is essential in our marriage, helping us remain anchored in God's promises. Psalm 100 reminds us to praise the Lord with gladness, to enter His presence with thanksgiving, and to recognize that His love endures forever. Praise is not just about worship—it is about trust, faith, and surrender.

Abraham demonstrated this understanding through his praise experiences. Wherever he went, he built altars, establishing formal places of worship. These altars were markers of God's faithfulness, reminders of His promises. We have embraced this principle by ensuring that our home is filled with praise and worship. Whether through prayer, music, or the simple act of speaking gratitude aloud, we set up signs of God's presence in our daily lives.

Abraham's faith was unwavering, even though he was a pilgrim in a foreign land. He praise because he believed that God would fulfill His promises, even when they seemed distant. Praise in marriage reflects this same principle—praising God in seasons of uncertainty strengthens faith and draws us closer to Him. We have learned that even when we do not see immediate answers to our prayers, worship keeps our hearts fixed on God's plan.

As a priest, Abraham had access to God, interceding for others. His encounter with Melchizedek demonstrated the significance of praise as fellowship with God, reinforcing that praise is not only personal but also communal. In our marriage, Kathleen and I integrate intercessory worship, praying for our family, community, and the world. Praise should not end with personal devotion—it must extend outward, standing in the gap for those in need.

Abraham took oaths in praising God with his worship, recognizing that God's covenant is unbreakable. Genesis and Hebrews show that these oaths were acts of deep commitment. In our relationship, praise is intertwined with our covenant of marriage. Praise binds us together, reminding us that just as God remains faithful to His people, we must remain faithful to Him and to each other.

The most profound act of worship Abraham displayed was offering Isaac. This moment in scripture highlights the heart of worship—offering to God what is most precious. True praise is about surrender, trusting that God's provision is greater than anything we could give. We apply this in our lives by ensuring that praise is not limited to words—it involves the surrender of our plans, expectations, and desires to God.

I witnessed the profound and transformative power of heaven unleashed while in Croatia. It was a lesson in trust, a testament to the strength found in praising God regardless of the circumstances.

One day, as I returned home from the city of Split, Croatia, a strange sensation enveloped me. Needles seemed to prick my skin, a haunting reminder of my childhood illness that had once left me paralyzed and unable to walk. The fear was palpable, but it was in this moment of vulnerability that heaven's power began to stir.

Kathleen, and I were alone in a foreign land, without family, friends, a doctor or even the comfort of familiar faces. Kathleen, an introvert by nature, had always been a graceful and quiet presence. For years, all through our speaking engagements before coming to Croatia and even after Croatia, she was known simply as Harrison's wife, a title that belied the depth of her spirit.

But as I lay incapacitated, unable to stand, something extraordinary happened. The Spirit of God ignited within Kathleen, transforming her into a vessel of divine power. For the first time in our years together, I saw her rise with a fervor that could only be described as heavenly.

She began to pray in the Spirit, her voice lifting in praise and commanding the forces of darkness to flee. She rebuked the sickness with authority, addressing the spirit that sought to cripple me. Her words were filled with conviction, declaring that we were missionaries sent by God, and that our work was far from finished.

Kathleen's desperation and unwavering faith opened the gates of heaven, unleashing a power that was both awe-inspiring and transformative. She grabbed my hands and, with a voice filled with divine authority, commanded me to walk in Jesus' name.

In that moment, I felt the blood flow through my body, a sensation reminiscent of the healing I experienced at fourteen years old. My body responded, the sickness dissipated, and I began to walk. The spirit of illness fled our home, never to return.

Throughout our time in Croatia and even upon our return to Canada, our family remained shielded from sickness, a testament to the protective power of God.

This experience reinforced a profound truth: when marked by God, no enemy can prevail against His divine protection. We are surrounded by the forces of heaven, supported by the Creator of all things. Every knee bows at the name of Jesus, who holds all resources and unleashes the power needed to fulfill His purpose.

Unleashing heaven's power is not merely an act; it is a journey of faith, trust, and unwavering praise. It is a reminder that in our moments of greatest need, heaven's power is ready to be unleashed, bringing healing, protection, and divine intervention.

As Kathleen prayed, her voice trembled with both desperation and unyielding faith. The room seemed to vibrate with a divine presence, as if the very walls bore witness to the battle between light and darkness. Her tears fell freely, each one a testament to her love and determination.

I remember the warmth of her hands as she held mine, her grip firm yet tender. Her eyes, usually so gentle, burned with a fierce resolve. In that moment, she was not just my wife; she was a warrior, wielding the power of heaven with every word she spoke.

The transformation was not just physical; it was deeply spiritual. As I took my first steps, I felt an overwhelming sense of peace and gratitude. The air in the room felt lighter, as if the weight of the sickness had been lifted and replaced with a tangible sense of hope and renewal.

This is a testament to the boundless power of faith and the miracles that unfold when we surrender to God's will. It is a story of love, resilience, and the unshakable belief that heaven's power is always within reach, ready to be unleashed in our darkest hours.

LAYING THE GROUNDWORK

Building a foundation of praise is more than a spiritual practice—it is a necessity for navigating life with peace, faith, and resilience. Kathleen and I have seen how prioritizing praise has shaped our family, sustained us through difficult seasons, and transformed the way we approach challenges. It is the groundwork we did building our family. Our journey has not always been easy, but praise has been the key to walking in confidence rather than fear, trusting in God's provision rather than living in anxiety.

When we first embarked on the mission field in Croatia from 1994 to 1997, we faced uncertainty at every turn. Moving to a foreign country, adjusting to new cultures, and stepping into the unknown required unwavering faith. We did not always have immediate answers or visible security, but we did have the power of praise. Praise became our refuge, our reminder that God was guiding our steps. There were days when we felt alone, when resources seemed scarce, but we refused to let fear dictate our mission. Instead, we praised. And time and again, God provided—doors opened, support arrived, and our calling was affirmed through His presence.

Raising seven children while serving in ministry was another challenge that required a deep foundation of praise. Parenthood itself is a journey of trust, but doing so while balancing the demands of leadership and service required divine strength. There were moments when financial concerns weighed on us, when exhaustion set in, and when we wondered if we could sustain the responsibilities we carried. But rather than panicking, we worshiped. We declared that God is our provider, our sustainer, and our guide. And He was faithful. Every one of our children, along with their spouses, serves the Lord today—not because of our perfect parenting but because our home was built on praise. Praise created an atmosphere where faith could flourish, where gratitude took priority over worry, and where trust replaced doubt.

Financial needs, employment concerns, and life's uncertainties have all been met through the power of praise. Worship is not about ignoring difficulties—it is about acknowledging that God is greater than them. Throughout Scripture, praise precedes breakthrough. When the Israelites needed provision in the wilderness, they were commanded to praise. When Paul and Silas were imprisoned, their praise led to their freedom. Praise is not reactive—it is proactive. It shifts the battle from the physical to the spiritual, inviting God to intervene where human efforts fall short.

Without a foundation of praise, fear dictates decisions, anxiety controls responses, and uncertainty becomes overwhelming. But when worship is present, peace reigns. We have chosen to make praise mandatory in our lives—not just as an act of devotion, but as the way we stand firm in faith. It has carried us through the unknown, sustained us in every season, and reinforced our trust in God's promises. Praise is not something we do occasionally—it is the foundation that keeps us grounded, connected, and walking in confidence.

Kathleen and I have learned that relationships, like towering buildings, require a strong foundation to endure life's pressures. Without a deep and reinforced base, even the most beautiful structures can crumble under the weight of challenges. We discovered that praise and worship serve as the anchor that keeps a relationship steady, allowing it to rise rather than fall when trials come.

When we first stepped into the mission field in Croatia from 1994 to 1997, uncertainty threatened to overwhelm us. We had no guarantees of financial support, no roadmap for what lay ahead, only faith that God had led us there for a purpose. There were moments when doubt crept in, when resources seemed insufficient, and when exhaustion took its toll. But instead of giving in to fear, we turned to praise. Praise became our refuge, the reminder that God had already gone before us. Every time we lifted our voices in song, we felt renewed strength, and time after time, provision arrived just when we needed it.

Raising seven children while walking the path of ministry was another journey that demanded unwavering trust. The weight of responsibility could have easily pulled us down into worry, but we chose worship instead. We saw miracles unfold—financial provision, unexpected opportunities, prayers answered in ways that left us in awe. Our children grew up in an atmosphere of praise, where praise was not reserved for Sunday mornings but was woven into the fabric of our daily lives. Each of them, along with their spouses, now serves the Lord. This was not the result of perfect parenting, but of building a foundation where God was always at the center.

A relationship without worship is like a building with shallow foundations. It may look strong on the surface, but the moment storms hit, cracks form, and the structure weakens. Praise reinforces love, trust, and resilience, ensuring that no matter how high a couple aims to go, they remain rooted in God's presence. Challenges will come—financial struggles, moments of doubt, unexpected losses—but a foundation of praise ensures that a marriage stands firm, unmoved by the winds of uncertainty.

We have seen how worship replaces anxiety with peace, how it silences fear and opens doors to divine provision. Praise is not just

LAYING THE GROUNDWORK

something we do—it is the very thing that holds us together, allowing us to rise, unshaken, through every season of life. And as long as we continue to build upon this foundation, we know that no trial will be greater than the God who sustains us.

Jesus made it clear when speaking to the Samaritan woman at the well that worship is not about location or tradition but must be done in spirit and in truth. This realization has shaped how we integrate praise and worship into our marriage. It is not about following rituals for the sake of appearances—it is about allowing our hearts to be fully engaged in honoring God. Praise happens in our conversations, in the way we support one another, and in the choices we make.

The Bible provides countless examples of praise and worship that transcend formality. Abel's sacrifice, the praise of angels, the faith of the centurion, and David's unashamed dance before the Lord all reflect praise as an outward declaration of faith. Kathleen and I have seen how praise affects our home environment. When we intentionally praise God—whether through music, prayer, or gratitude—it shifts our perspective, reminding us that love is sustained by faith.

Praise is one of the most powerful ways to engage in worship. Scripture frequently commands us to "praise the Lord," not as an obligation but as a natural response to His goodness. We have seen firsthand how praise shifts the atmosphere in our home. Whether through music, spoken gratitude, or the quiet recognition of God's presence, praise sets the tone for faith. It acknowledges His character and His actions, reminding us that He is worthy of adoration. Much like cheering at a ball game comes instinctively, worship should feel just as natural when recognizing the victories God has won for us.

Scripture reading is another essential element of praise, both in church and in personal devotion. In older churches, two pulpits were used—one for preaching and another for reading the Word aloud, honouring the tradition of declaring scripture publicly. We have

AS FOR ME AND MY SPOUSE WE WILL PRAISE THE LORD

embraced this principle in our own lives, ensuring that scripture remains at the center of our faith. Reading the Bible daily, respecting its truth, and applying its wisdom keeps us aligned with God's will. The ancient Israelites were commanded to post scripture on their walls, a reminder that God's word should be ever-present in our hearts and homes.

Praise influences how we treat one another. It teaches patience, kindness, and humility, reinforcing the biblical truth that love is more than emotion—it is a reflection of God's character. We rely on praise to keep our marriage rooted in peace. When frustration arises, praise reminds us to shift our focus from the problem to the Provider.

Praise requires intentionality. They do not happen by accident—they are cultivated, nurtured, and prioritized. We weave praise into our daily routine because we know it is what keeps our faith alive and our love strong. Praise is not an obligation—it is the foundation of joy, the rhythm of faith, and the safeguard of peace in our lives.

Tithing is an act of praise and worship that reflects trust in God's provision. The practice of giving a tenth of what we have dates back to Abraham, signifying surrender and faith. Kathleen and I have learned that tithing is not just about financial giving—it is about recognizing God's blessings, practicing good stewardship, and honouring Him in tangible ways. Giving reflects gratitude, acknowledging that everything we have comes from Him.

Prayer is another cornerstone of praise. Volumes have been written about its significance, but at its core, prayer is how we communicate with God. Public prayer expresses dependence on His strength, acknowledges our sins, and intercedes for others. We have built prayer into our daily routine, understanding that it is the direct line to God's presence. Praying together strengthens our relationship, bringing unity, peace, and divine guidance.

Communion is one of the most sacred elements of praise, representing Christ's sacrifice for our sins. It is a moment of self-examination, reminding us to reflect on our hearts, repent, and seek renewal. We recognize the importance of approaching communion with humility, ensuring that our faith is aligned with God's truth. Communion reminds us of our unity—just as Christ's body was one, the church must remain united. It also reinforces the hope of resurrection, proclaiming our belief in Christ's return and the promise of eternal life.

Forgiveness is central to praise. Repentance allows us to receive forgiveness, but worship also calls us to extend that grace to others. Kathleen and I strive to practice forgiveness in our marriage, recognizing that just as Christ bore the consequences of our sins, we must be willing to let go of grievances and show mercy.

True worship changes everything. It touches how we praise, how we trust, how we forgive, and how we proclaim the gospel. We continue to build our lives on the foundation of praise, knowing that it is what keeps us grounded in faith, connected in love, and steadfast in God's presence.

We discovered something powerful in our journey together—praise and worship became our refuge, our way of keeping peace alive even in the most mundane moments. It started with a simple choice. Instead of letting frustration take control during difficult conversations, especially while driving, we began singing together. What began as a way to diffuse tension became a sacred rhythm in our relationship, one that has transformed the way we experience love, faith, and unity.

Driving together used to be an arena for disagreements. One of us would say something in the heat of the moment, the other would respond, and suddenly, the atmosphere in the car would shift from peace to frustration. But then, something changed. One day, instead of letting an argument escalate, Kathleen started singing. I hesitated at first, but then joined in, and soon, the tension dissolved as we found harmony—not just in the music, but in our hearts.

We didn't just sing—we allowed creativity and joy to guide us. We experimented with harmonizing, stretching melodies, blending our voices, making the act of worship personal and unique. It wasn't about performance; it was about surrender. The car transformed from a place of potential conflict into a moving sanctuary where the presence of God overtook us. We weren't just singing songs—we were inviting peace into our relationship, submitting our worries and frustrations to God, knowing that everything would be okay.

There was something incredibly freeing about worshiping together in such an unexpected place. It reminded us that praise is our life, something natural, something that bridged the emotional and spiritual gaps that sometimes form in marriage. When we sang, our voices weren't just merging—they were declaring unity, trust, and faith.

As time passed, this practice became second nature to us. We didn't wait for problems to arise before singing; it became the soundtrack of our journeys together. Praise wasn't just tools to fix something—they became the foundation for deeper connection. It helped us communicate in ways words never could, strengthened our emotional bond, and reminded us that marriage is not just about two people navigating life—it is about keeping God at the center.

Now, when we drive, our first instinct is to sing. It is no longer about avoiding arguments—it is about maintaining the presence of God wherever we go. Praise and Worship has rewired how we engage with each other, replaced tension with tranquility, and given us a deep spiritual bond that echoes beyond melody and lyrics. It is a reminder that, no matter the journey, God is with us, leading, guiding, and ensuring that we always find harmony—not just in our voices, but in our hearts.

LAYING THE GROUNDWORK

AS FOR ME AND MY SPOUSE WE WILL PRAISE THE LORD!

The early years of our marriage were simple yet sacred—marked by quiet moments of devotion and the ever-present reality of struggle. Kathleen and I started out in a modest little house in the countryside, a three-bedroom home nestled on a farm, costing us only $250 a month. It wasn't grand, but it was ours. It was where we built the foundation of our life together, where faith was tested, and where the calling to serve was first planted deep within us.

Kathleen had just graduated from school and we both were working at a group home for men and women who are developmental delayed. I, also spent my days supporting men with acquired brain injuries and other challenges. We were young, in love, and filled with a desire to help others—but the weight of life, the questions of purpose, and the hardships that come with walking a path of faith were never far behind.

There were times when frustration crept in—times when we felt abandoned, misunderstood, and uncertain. The mission of bringing Christ's love to others was easy to lose sight of when bills piled up and exhaustion settled into our bones. It would have been easy to turn away, to let disappointment taint our hearts. But something within us—

perhaps the gentle whisper of the Lord, perhaps the prayers we murmured in the stillness of the night—kept us anchored.

One moment in particular stands out like a beacon, guiding our steps even now. I had found myself in my boss's office on a day when she wasn't there. Playfully, perhaps curiously, I sat in her chair, propping my feet on her desk, wondering what it felt like to be in a position of leadership. It was an innocent act—one of curiosity rather than ambition.

And then she walked in.

She stood in the doorway, the light behind her casting a soft glow around her silhouette. Her voice was firm but gentle as she asked, "What do you want for your life?"

The words struck me with an unexpected force. It wasn't just a question; it felt like an invitation—an opportunity to speak out the deepest longing of my heart. I barely had time to think before the words poured out.

"I want to go to Bible school. I want to serve people."

In that moment, I knew. It wasn't just my voice answering her—it was the Lord stirring within me, pulling me toward a greater purpose. And that moment became a turning point, a catalyst for the life Kathleen and I would build together.

We learned quickly that marriage wasn't just about companionship—it was about partnership in faith. The struggles we faced as a couple were not just burdens to bear; they were mountains to climb, and prayer became the rope that pulled us forward. When we knelt together in worship, when we lifted our hands in praise, something remarkable happened—spiritual resiliency strengthened us, making us unshakable.

AS FOR ME AND MY SPOUSE WE WILL PRAISE THE LORD

We refused to let life's disappointments harden our hearts against God. Instead, we surrendered every frustration, every doubt, and every fear into His hands. And in return, He filled our home with peace.

Through every trial, through every moment where it seemed easier to walk away than to persevere, we chose to stay—firm in our commitment, unwavering in our service. Because as for me and my spouse, we will serve the Lord.

And that choice—the daily decision to love, to forgive, to pray, and to walk faithfully—has carried us through every season.

When we made the decision to go to Bible school, it felt like stepping into the unknown—both exciting and daunting. The school was over an hour away from our little country home, and the financial burden loomed over us like a question waiting to be answered. But we knew one thing for certain: If God wanted us there, He would make a way.

So, we prayed. I told God that if He desired this path for us, He would need to provide a home where we wouldn't pay more than $250 a month in rent and utilities. It seemed impossible, yet faith has always danced on the edge of impossibility.

Not long after that prayer, Kathleen and I applied for a three-bedroom apartment just a few kilometers away from the Bible school. When we sat down for an interview with the property manager, we had no idea what God was about to do. By the end of our conversation, they offered us the apartment for $247 a month—utilities included. Not just the basics, but everything: cable, hydro, and water.

The moment we heard the news, Kathleen and I lifted our hands to the heavens, praising God for His faithfulness. It was more than just an apartment—it was confirmation. It was God saying, "I am with you."

That little apartment became the center of our life for over fifteen years. A safe haven, a place of prayer, a home where the foundation of our ministry deepened. Even when life pulled us across the world—

spending several years in Croatia during the war from 1994 to 1997—we never lost sight of God's provision. Someone lived in our apartment while we were away, and when we returned, it was still waiting for us, as if God had held it in His hands all along.

Then came another leap of faith.

In 1999, we felt God calling us to Toronto, Ontario, and this time, the step was bigger. We were leaving the security of our small apartment for a four-bedroom house—a home we knew, by earthly standards, we weren't qualified to purchase. But favour isn't measured by worldly qualifications. It was God who placed this opportunity before us, and He paved the way through the heart of the homeowner.

The realtor told her we were pastors, that we were planting a church in the city. And she—moved not by numbers or logic, but by something deeper—sold us the house.

Suddenly, our mortgage leapt from $247 a month to $1,700. Utility costs, food, taxes, insurance, and the needs of seven children—we were stretched beyond reason. On paper, none of it made sense. But faith doesn't live on paper.

We pastored a church that carried a debt of over $33,000, ran a Bible school for ten years that also battled financial strain, paid $2,500 a month for the church building and $1,500 for the school rental. By all calculations, we should not have been able to survive.

But God.

Even now, when we look back, we can't explain how every bill was paid. How we managed with only $22,000 annual income while raising seven children. How we kept going when all odds pointed toward failure. The only explanation is that the Lord stretched our resources in a way that defied logic. A five-dollar bill seemed to stretch into fifty. Miracles whispered through our finances, carrying us step by step until, one day, the debt was gone, and we moved into a bigger house—a six-bedroom home that held not only our growing family but the undeniable evidence of God's provision.

We learned that faith isn't just about believing—it's about walking forward when every step seems impossible, when logic tells you to turn back. It's about trusting in God's abundance, even when your hands are empty.

And so, as for me and my spouse, we will serve the Lord.

No matter the cost. No matter the challenge.

Because the One who calls us is always faithful.

We would throw our hands up to the heavens and praise the Lord, knowing that what seemed impossible for us was always possible with Him. Praise wasn't just something we did—it was the very weapon we wielded against discouragement, against doubt, against every obstacle that stood in our way. Victory after victory, breakthrough after breakthrough—our praise carried us through every storm.

There were moments when life tried to shake us, when financial strain, exhaustion, and uncertainty pressed against us, threatening to distract us from the calling God had placed on our lives. But one thing we knew—praise was our strength. It was the force that anchored our souls in truth, that lifted our eyes from the struggle and fixed them firmly on the One who never fails.

It reminds me of the story of Jesus and His disciples on the Sea of Galilee after performing countless miracles. The Bible tells us that a violent storm arose, and the disciples, though they had seen Jesus do the impossible, began to panic. Their boat was rocking, and fear gripped their hearts, making them certain they would perish.

But Jesus—calm, unwavering—was asleep. He wasn't worried about the wind, the waves, or the chaos around Him. The disciples, frantic, woke Him, and in an instant, He rebuked the storm. The wind ceased. The waters calmed. Peace replaced fear.

And yet, the story didn't end there.

Their journey had a purpose. On the other side of that storm, a man in desperate need awaited them—a man tormented, possessed, uncontrollable, unable to be bound by chains. He ran wild, naked, screaming in agony, as demons tore at his soul. But when he saw Jesus, he knew. He recognized the Son of God. And in that moment, he pleaded to be set free.

Jesus didn't come merely to still the storm on the water—He came to still the storm within that man. He cast the demons into a herd of pigs, and in an instant, the man was delivered.

That story teaches us something powerful—there will always be storms. The wind will rage, the waves will threaten to pull us under. But if we fix our eyes on Jesus, if we refuse to let fear distract us from our mission, if we worship through the storm instead of succumbing to it, we will see victory.

Kathleen and I learned this firsthand. When the weight of life pressed in, when our circumstances screamed that it was impossible, we praised anyway. We worshiped before the breakthrough, before the provision, before we saw the evidence of God's hand moving.

And time after time, He carried us through.

We have no doubt that praise to God and worship were the strength we carried into every battle. They were the songs that sustained us, the declarations that lifted our weary hearts, the promises we clung to when the storm seemed too great.

Just as Jesus stayed focused on His assignment, we stayed focused on ours—to serve the Lord, to trust in His provision, and to never allow

AS FOR ME AND MY SPOUSE WE WILL PRAISE THE LORD

life's circumstances to pull us away from what we knew He had planned for us.

And because of that, victory was ours.

Faithful as He has always been, God continued to move, to provide, to make a way where there seemed to be none. And through it all, our praise never wavered.

For as long as we live, we will praise the Lord.

And we will worship Him every step of the way.

In your marriage, there will be distractions—storms that arise unexpectedly, moments that test your patience and your faith. But in the midst of those storms, you must lift your hands to heaven and praise the Lord. Worship is more than just a melody; it is a force, a divine atmosphere that invites God's presence to dwell in your home, in your relationship, in every step you take together. It is through this sacred act of surrender that the Holy Spirit leads your path, carrying you toward the assignment He has prepared for you.

We have seen time and again the power of praise shaping our lives. We have witnessed God's hands working in ways that defy logic, His favour carrying us through challenges that seemed impossible to overcome. But the key was always the atmosphere we created in our marriage—one where the Holy Spirit was at the center, where His voice was louder than any doubt, where His presence was the foundation upon which we raised our family of seven children.

If you desire to see God move powerfully in your life, if you long for a marriage strengthened beyond measure, if you want victory in the face of conflict and confusion, there is one simple yet profound truth to embrace: Stop what you are doing and start praising the Lord.

Praise breaks chains. It shifts perspectives. It silences fear, extinguishes doubt, and dismantles pride. It transforms a weary heart

AS FOR ME AND MY SPOUSE WE WILL PRAISE THE LORD!

into one full of joy, replaces uncertainty with confidence, and infuses a home with the unwavering assurance that the God of creation stands beside you.

Kathleen and I have seen this firsthand—the miraculous ways God moves when His people choose worship over worry, when they allow His presence to consume them rather than the burdens of life.

The storms may come, but they do not have the power to shake what is anchored in Him.

So we will continue to serve the Lord.

And we will continue to praise Him—knowing that with Him, victory is always within reach.

A MARRIAGE ROOTED IN PRAISE

In marriage, life will bring distractions. There will be storms that shake your foundation, moments where doubt creeps in, and seasons that challenge your faith. But the key to navigating these trials is found in one profound practice—praise. When storms rise, when circumstances feel overwhelming, lifting your hands in worship transforms the atmosphere. Praise invites God's presence into your marriage, and it becomes the force that sustains and strengthens you.

Kathleen and I built our marriage on praise and worship. It was not a ritual or an obligation—it was our lifeline. Every trial that came our way, every financial struggle, every difficult decision, we met with praise. We refused to let circumstances dictate our faith, because we knew that God's plans for us were greater than any challenge we faced. Praise has been our weapon against discouragement, and in His presence, we found clarity, strength, and resilience.

We see God's hand move in countless ways. From the provision of our first home to the financial miracles that kept our family thriving, we witnessed time and time again how His presence transformed impossibilities into victories. But it wasn't just about the moments when we saw breakthrough—it was about surrendering to Him even when

A MARRIAGE ROOTED IN PRAISE

there were no answers. Worship wasn't just an act of gratitude when things went well; it was our declaration of trust when life felt uncertain.

In our home, we cultivate an atmosphere of praise. We spoke words of life over each other, we prayed together, we invited the Holy Spirit to guide our steps. It was this foundation that allowed us to raise seven children, to continue pastoring, to walk boldly in the assignment God had given us. Without His presence in our marriage, the weight of life could have easily pulled us apart. But with Him at the center, we stood firm.

If you want to see the power of God working in your marriage, if you desire unity, peace, and strength in the midst of difficulty, you must create an atmosphere where His presence dwells. Praise is the daily practice of inviting God into your marriage, your home, your conversations. It transforms your relationship, allowing spiritual resiliency to take root.

When conflict arises, when confusion clouds your thoughts, when burdens feel too heavy, stop what you're doing and begin to praise. You will be amazed at how quickly everything shifts. Fear will fade. Doubt will dissolve. Worry and pride will lose their grip. In place of these things, joy will rise, confidence will be restored, and stability will take hold in your heart, reminding you that the Creator of the universe stands with you.

Marriage is not just about companionship—it is about partnership in faith. It is about walking together in purpose, knowing that you are called not just to love each other, but to serve the Lord as one. And when God is at the center, when worship is your foundation, there is nothing that can shake what He has built in you.

This is how we stand strong. This is how we move forward in faith. This is how we remain victorious. Because as for me and my spouse, we will praise the Lord. And we will praise Him, always.

AS FOR ME AND MY SPOUSE WE WILL PRAISE THE LORD

Unlike most couples, Kathleen and I met not in the ordinary rush of life, but in a sacred space—within the walls of the church, where faith and worship formed the foundation of our lives. It was April 1989, a crisp spring evening, and I had just finished speaking at a service when I saw her. There was something radiant about her, something warm and familiar, as though God Himself had placed her in my path with divine intention.

Feeling bold in the moment, I walked up to her after the service and asked if she would join me on a visit to the hospital to pray for the sick, something I often did on weekends. It was how I lived out my faith—not just in words but in action. But instead of going to the hospital, we found ourselves at a young adult roller-skating event. And that night, something remarkable happened. As I clumsily lost my footing and tumbled to the ground, Kathleen reached down to pull me up. That simple touch ignited something inexplicable within me, and in that instant, the Holy Spirit whispered: *She is your wife.*

I wasn't sure if I was laughing because I had just fallen or because of the voice I had heard. Either way, my heart knew.

Two days later, we had dinner together. After our meal, we took a quiet stroll near the lake, lost in conversation. And then, as if orchestrated by heaven, our eyes fell upon two swans—one black, one white—gliding effortlessly across the water. Was it another sign? A reflection of two lives about to merge, beautifully distinct yet perfectly complementary? In that moment, the peace of the Lord settled deep within me.

Within four months, we were engaged and a year later on August 11, 1990, surrounded by friends, family, and the tangible presence of the Holy Spirit, we stood before the altar and vowed our lives to each other—with praise, worship, and gratitude. Unlike any wedding I had ever witnessed, ours was saturated in praise and thanksgiving, a testimony to the goodness of God.

A MARRIAGE ROOTED IN PRAISE

This is the life we have chosen—to praise the Lord from earth into eternity. Every season, every trial, every victory is marked by His hand. We have seen His goodness chase after us. We have felt His presence even in moments of discouragement. We rejoice as all our children serve the Lord alongside their spouses, knowing that His promises remain steadfast.

No matter what comes, we cling to the truth that He orders our steps. His word is a lamp unto our feet, a light unto our path. He will never leave us nor forsake us. We are inscribed in the palms of His hands.

And so, we will praise Him—not just for what He has done, but for what He is yet to do. Even when things don't unfold the way we expect, we trust Him fully, knowing that He works all things together for our good.

CONCLUSION

As the final pages of this book turn, our journey of praise continues. It does not end here, nor is it confined to the words printed on these pages. It stretches beyond time, beyond circumstance, beyond every trial and triumph we have walked through. Worship is the very breath of our marriage, the foundation upon which we have built our lives. It has carried us through storms, sustained us through uncertainty, and drawn us ever closer to the heart of God.

Looking back, I am overwhelmed by the goodness of the Lord—not because our path has been easy, but because His presence has been steadfast. There were times when praise came naturally, when joy was abundant, when gratitude flowed effortlessly from our lips. But there were also moments when worship required strength, when faith was tested, when lifting our voices was an act of surrender rather than celebration. Through it all, praise has remained our refuge, our weapon, our unwavering declaration that God is good, no matter the season.

I think of the times when grief threatened to steal our joy—when sorrow sat heavily in our hearts and the silence of loss echoed louder than the voice of hope. The passing of my dear friend Tihomir was one of those moments. His absence left a void that words could not fill, and in that season of mourning, I wrestled with the weight of pain. Yet, even

CONCLUSION

in grief, praise found its way through. Worship does not always require understanding; it simply calls for trust. And so, even in the quiet ache of loss, we lifted our hands, not because it was easy, but because God remained faithful.

Faith has also been tested in the face of fear. Living as Protestants in Croatia presented its own unique challenges—moments of unease, times when opposition felt tangible. Yet, through every trial, praise became a shield, a declaration that fear would not have the final word. Worship is not just a melody sung in church; it is a battle cry, a weapon against discouragement, a proclamation of God's sovereignty. We learned to stand firm, not because we were strong, but because He was.

I reflect on our journey, on the places we have walked through—both physically and spiritually. I remember returning from India, only to find our van stolen, along with the precious carved elephants we had brought back. Frustration clouded my mind, disappointment tempted my heart to withdraw. It would have been easy to question, easy to give in to resentment. But worship reminds us that God is bigger than our circumstances. He is not defined by loss, nor limited by human understanding. And so, even in frustration, we chose to praise.

Then came the days when sickness knocked at our door, when my body weakened and my spirit wavered. I watched Kathleen stand strong, her faith unwavering as she called down heaven to rescue us. It was in those moments that I saw the power of praise—not only in shifting our hearts but in shifting the very atmosphere. Worship has never been just about emotion; it is about transformation. When we lift our voices in faith, even when we do not yet see the breakthrough, heaven moves.

Through every valley and mountaintop, one truth has remained unchanged—God is worthy of our praise. Not because life has been perfect, but because He has been constant. Not because we have always understood His ways, but because we trust His heart. There is nothing that can steal His goodness, no trial that can undo His promises.

AS FOR ME AND MY SPOUSE WE WILL PRAISE THE LORD

And so, as we close this chapter, as we reflect on all He has done, our declaration remains steadfast: *As for me and my spouse, we will praise the Lord.*

This book is not just a story of our lives, but an invitation to every heart that reads these words. It is a call to trust in the goodness of God, to hold fast to His promises, to worship in every season. There will be days when praise is effortless, when thanksgiving flows without hesitation. But there will also be days when worship must rise above struggle, when faith must fight to believe. In both, God is present. In both, He is worthy.

To those who turn this final page, may you find encouragement in these words. May you be reminded that no matter where you stand—whether in the valley of loss or on the mountaintop of victory—God is near. His love surrounds you, His mercy sustains you, His faithfulness never wavers. May your own journey be marked by the power of worship, the strength of surrender, the unwavering trust that God is working all things together for good.

Praise is not just a response to blessing. It is a declaration in the midst of uncertainty, a surrender in the face of struggle, a confident assurance that even when we do not see, God is still moving. Worship is the sound of heaven, the anthem of faith, the language of hope. And in every breath, in every moment, through every trial and triumph, may we all find the courage to lift our voices and declare His goodness.

We will continue to praise Him. In every step we take, in every day we are given, our hearts will lift His name high. Not because life is always easy, but because we know that through it all, He is faithful. He is worthy. He is good.

And so, now and forevermore, we declare: *As for me and my spouse, we will praise the Lord!*

THE END!

www.ingramcontent.com/pod-product-compliance
Lightning Source LLC
Chambersburg PA
CBHW050341010526
44119CB00049B/651